THE PUBLIC IS NEVER WRONG

THE PUBLIC IS NEVER WRONG

THE AUTOBIOGRAPHY OF

Adolph Zukor

WITH DALE KRAMER

G. P. Putnam's Sons New York

Published on the same day in the Dominion of Canada by Thomas Allen, Ltd., Toronto.

Library of Congress Catalog Card Number: 53-8164

MANUFACTURED IN THE UNITED STATES OF AMERICA

VAN REES PRESS • NEW YORK

To my wife,

LOTTIE

Illustrations

THE PUBLIC IS NEVER WRONG

1

A WHILE ago people began to say to me that it was high time I wrote my memoirs. A man's eightieth birthday and his half century's anniversary in an industry as comparatively new and turbulent as the movies, was, they argued, a good vantage point from which to cast his eyes backward and jot down a record of events which would be of interest to readers and valuable to historians.

My enthusiasm did not catch fire. In the first place, I get down to work early in the morning, either at my Paramount offices in New York or at the Paramount studios in Hollywood. A man is kept busy enough wrestling current matters and plotting the future without reliving the past. And at that particular moment, while funeral orations were being delivered over the film industry, we were secretly experimenting with three-dimensional pictures, wide screens, and other items calculated to prove that the reports of our death were grossly exaggerated.

Furthermore, I said, people are interested in screen personalities, mainly the stars. It was that belief, after all, on which I banked everything with my first company, Famous Players in Famous Plays, more than forty years ago. It had been my contention that audiences would sit through feature-length films starring the great theater figures. Makers and exhibitors of the one-reelers and occasional two-reelers—all there were at the time—had not been able to make up their minds whether the lunatic asylum or the poorhouse would get me first. But audiences did sit through them.

My supreme faith was in the public, as it is today. I was convinced further that the audiences would create stars of its own. The one-reelers of the period around 1910 were identifying a little maiden with golden curls simply as "Little Mary." Picturemakers feared that player billing would lead to demands for wages of more than a few dollars a week.

To this day Mary Pickford—she was the little girl with the curls—and I grow sentimental remembering the night, after she had come to work for me in feature pictures, that we stood together and looked at her name in bright lights on a theater marquee. Mary often called me Papa Zukor, her own father having died in her infancy. That night she put her head on my shoulder and wept. My eyes were not dry either. Mary and I went a long way together, and when we parted—a million-odd-dollars-a-year salary was all I felt I should pay—we were as good friends as ever.

Mary Pickford was the first of the great stars. We built the modern movie industry on the star system, but the public made the stars. All the skill of directors and all the booming of press-agent drums will not make a star. Only the audiences can do it. Some quality of the player—often elusive—is translated by the screen to the audience.

We study audience reactions with great care. Once we know what is going on there are many things we can do to help the player to stardom. Naturally we do our best, for we know that, while many other factors are important, the movie industry's foundation is still the star system.

And so, regarding the suggestion for writing my memoirs, I pointed out that the public is interested in the glamorous players, not the figures behind the screen.

A friend to whom I expounded this view agreed only in part. He is a man not noted for reverence. "Why," he said, "I saw you described in a newspaper only the other day as a movie mogul. It happens all the time, except that sometimes you are a cinema tycoon or perhaps the Old Napoleon. I've seen you described as a caliph, and even, in a respected history book, as a wild Sioux Indian ghost dancer striking terror into the hearts of the enemy."

"Oh," I said, "in this industry superlatives are not unknown. I never did pay much attention to what people called me. Don't yet."

"Lately," he went on, "I've been reading fictional accounts of the early moviemakers. All of them apparently wild and flamboyant characters mixed up in some mighty weird goings on."

"Colorful, a lot of them," I admitted. "Showmen. You had to be a showman. But those who survived were level-headed too. I could name—"

"All right." He waved me down. "Likely enough the

real people, the real events, had more drama, more color, than the writers are able to make up. Seems to me they're writing a lot of fiction about stars too. You've known the moguls and the stars since the year one. If the public likes the fiction, then it wants facts. How about Rudolph Valentino? There was a colorful one. Weren't you a pall-bearer at that celebrated funeral of his where the women rioted?"

I handed him a cigar, since it was plain that he had no intention of going away. "Yes. But the big commotion was while he lay in state a day or two earlier. Did I ever tell you about our lunch a week before he died? Strange thing—"

"Save it for the book," my friend said, lighting up. "How about Doug Fairbanks?"

"Always fond of him," I said, "even though his court-ship of Mary Pickford was a worry to me. Both tech-nically still married to others, you know. Bad publicity might have ruined her career, maybe his too."

My friend nodded. "William S. Hart was a pal of yours."

"Well," I said, warming up a little, "there's a more colorful fellow off the screen than on, if that's the sort of thing you're driving at."

He continued, "How about Gloria Swanson, Pola Negri?"

"Oh, yes. They fought it out for queen of the studio. We had some fine actresses earlier—Marguerite Clark, Pauline Frederick, Marie Doro, Mable Normand. Back even farther were Sarah Bernhardt, Lily Langtry, Minnie Maddern Fiske. But all that was a long time ago."

"Never mind," said my friend. "People rising forty remember and anyhow you have to go way back to make sense out of the present. What about the male stars?"

I ran them over in my mind. "John Barrymore forty years ago. Wally Reid, a heartbreaking tragedy. Tommy Meighan was like one of my family. Charles Ray, Adolphe Menjou. And of course Mack Sennett and his comedians were associated with us. We brought Emil Jannings from Germany and Maurice Chevalier from France. Chevalier was another one who seemed a part of my family."

"All right," my friend said, ticking off on his fingers, "you had Mary Pickford, the sweet little ingénue, and Doug Fairbanks, the dazzling jumper, and you made *The Sheik* which set off the Valentino craze. All created or anyhow fitted national eras of a sort. How about Flaming Youth and the Jazz Age?"

"Clara Bow," I said. "We made the picture *It* and of course Clara became the 'It' girl. That was in the twenties. We brought Marlene Dietrich over and she fit the thirties better. So did Claudette Colbert."

"Mae West?"

"When you speak of eras, I'd say Mae was in command during the depression years. Mae surprised us, and maybe herself. But Mae knew her talents in relation to the audiences—which is always what counts—better than we did."

My friend's cigar was growing short and he crushed it out. "Sounds like you'll do. What with some of the later figures—Gary Cooper, Carole Lombard, William Powell, Bing Crosby, Bob Hope, and so forth—you have plenty of stars to talk about. The Bill Boyd-Hopalong Cassidy story you told me one time illustrates the strange twists which audience reactions sometimes cause. And you can work in the moguls."

I thrust the opened cigar box at him. "Now, you started this, and I better tell you right here and now that I can't match up to the fiction on your so-called moguls. The mogul has been played up as a kind of lavish potentate surrounded by flunkies. Now I suppose Marcus Loew would come under the mogul heading. He put together a theater empire and in due course the Metro-Goldwyn-Mayer producing company. But, frankly, I always thought of Marcus as more of a tennis mogul. He nearly always beat me."

"You always claimed to be a pretty good athlete."

"Boxer," I said, lighting one of the five daily cigars I have rationed myself down to, "maybe you haven't noticed my cauliflower ear before. And baseball catcher. That accounts for this stiff finger. But I never boxed Marcus—he was too big and anyhow we were a little past the boxing prime when we first knew each other well."

That set me off on an account of our tennis matches, to which my friend listened with, for him, reasonably good grace. We played hard—when we could keep our faces straight. Trouble was that we usually played with Lew Fields, of the celebrated comic team of Weber & Fields, and Sam Bernard, another great dialect comedian. They were as funny on the court as on the stage, or funnier.

You'd go to hit the ball, one of them would crack a joke in whatever dialect suited his purpose, and the racket was likely to fall out of your hand.

It was true, I pointed out, that I once came off winner in a sort of athletic contest with Marcus, though he looked the better of the two after it was over. My daughter married his son, and we heard about the birth of our first mutual grandchild while together in Chicago. On the train coming back we laid a bet on who would be first to reach the hospital. The trained pulled into New York early in the morning. Marcus took time to shave. I didn't and beat him.

"So you can see," I told my friend, "that I can't turn up the expected kind of mogul stories. Take another example. Certainly Joe Schenck, a founder of Twentieth Century-Fox, gets the mogul rating. I'm more likely to think of him as the joke partner of Sid Grauman, the greatest practical joker of them all. Come to think of it, though, Joe may have had caliph ambitions. I always suspected that he helped Grauman spirit the oriental rug from the lobby of the old Alexandria Hotel in Los Angeles—the early hangout of movie people—in broad daylight. The straight of how it was managed never did come out. Maybe the Oriental rug gave Grauman the idea for his Oriental and Chinese theaters, or the other way around. I don't know how he got the idea of having movie people make footprints in his cement. I wouldn't have dared do it while Sid was alive. He'd have figured out a way to get me stuck in the cement."

My mind continued to delve into the past, which may have been my friend's purpose to begin with. Before long I was telling him about the late round-table dinners some of us used to eat nearly half a century ago at Shanley's Restaurant at Forty-third Street and Broadway, where the Paramount building and theater stand now. Shanley's was a theatrical rendezvous, much like the Sardi's of today. From half a dozen to a dozen of us would gather between eleven o'clock and midnight, eat, and sit up to all hours building castles in the air.

When we began to meet at Shanley's none of us was over forty. Not unless it was William A. Brady, and he couldn't have been much older, though he had a fascinating career behind him. He had managed Gentleman Jim Corbett and Jim Jeffries, the heavyweight champions. At the time I speak of, Brady, a big handsome fellow, was devoting all his time to theatrical productions. Each of us had his pet dream, and Brady's was to step into the theatrical producing class of David Belasco and the Frohmans, Charles and Daniel.

A couple of the younger regulars—Jake and Lee Shubert—had come down from Syracuse and were fighting Klaw & Erlanger, the legitimate theatrical syndicate. The Shuberts had suffered a big loss when their brother Sam was killed in a train accident. They were head over heels in theatrical production as well as in property but they didn't consider movies as being quite so despicable as most stage people did. The Shuberts were full of vim, and still are.

There was our other pair of brothers, Joe and Nick

Schenck. They had moved from the drugstore business in the Bronx to management of an amusement park, which occupied only part of their time. Marcus Loew, seeing great possibilities in the Schenck boys, was making places for them in his enterprises. Joe booked vaudeville acts. Nick devoted most of his time to theater management. Many years later he followed Loew into movie production and, after Loew's death, became head of Metro-Goldwyn-Mayer, as he is today.

Thus seven of the round-table regulars were in the business end—Brady, the Shuberts, the Schencks, Marcus Loew, and myself. I had moved from the fur business to penny arcades and then into movie and vaudeville theater operation. In some of the ventures I was associated with Loew and in some with Brady.

My dream was to make feature-length pictures to replace the one- and two-reelers. Table rules allowed a man to talk about his dream. But no one took me very seriously. Movies were regarded at that table, as by most of the public, as a thin cut above burlesque and well below cheap vaudeville.

Our round table was graced also by actors. Among them was David Warfield, a great stage favorite, one of Belasco's stars. At the same time he was a shrewd businessman who invested in the theater business. Joe Weber, the other half of the Weber & Fields team, was often on hand, along with Fields. Both had theatrical enterprises aside from their stage appearances. We couldn't have gotten along, of course, without that other comedian, Sam Bernard. A fellow could tour his theaters, catch disappointing acts, count poor houses, and know that Bernard would be at Shanley's to dispel the gloom.

One incident sticks in my mind as illustrating the lowly place of the movies at the time. Marcus Loew had converted a burlesque house in Brooklyn for exclusive showing of movies. There may have been a "store" theater—a vacant store with a few chairs—or two, but I think this was the first bona-fide theater in Brooklyn devoted to the movies.

The night of the opening we waited at Shanley's for a report.

Loew came in, and his large eyes were somber. "One ticket sold all day," he announced. "Gross receipts, ten cents."

"Maybe," suggested Bernard, "your admission price was too high."

"Well, we gave the dime back," Loew said. "The customer was an old woman. We ran the picture and returned her money."

Eventually the Brooklyn theater—I think it was called the Royal—more than paid its way. But Loew's faith in pictures was shaken and remained so for a long time.

By remarking on the ill repute of early motion pictures I do not mean to deprecate the struggles of pioneers in the new and crude medium before my inauguration of the feature-length picture in America. Quite the opposite.

One could not pay too much tribute to those early directing geniuses, David Wark Griffith and Edwin S. Porter, who were forging a motion picture technique.

Porter's *The Great Train Robbery* is mentioned whenever film history is discussed. Porter was to become my partner in launching feature pictures and later I was closely associated with Griffith.

In those early days adventurous young men went into film-making in much the same spirit others joined the gold rush. As a matter of fact, Jesse L. Lasky, one of the great figures, had been in the Alaska rush before entering films. Cecil B. De Mille has told me that it was nip and tuck with him whether to go into picturemaking or join a revolution somewhere south of the border.

De Mille and Lasky were eating dinner in the Claridge Grill one night, depressed and financially bent. De Mille, a son of playwright Henry Churchill De Mille, had recently directed a play which the public had not cherished. Lasky, a former cornet player in a family vaudeville act as well as gold hunter, had opened a plush cabaret. He is credited with bringing the cabaret to America, but he seems to have been ahead of his time. It failed.

"Perhaps," De Mille said, " we had better go down to Mexico and join a revolution."

Lasky had a different idea. "If it's excitement you want," he said, "let's make moving pictures."

They turned over a menu and began to form a company.

Sam Goldfish (later Sam Goldwyn) came into the restaurant, and it could readily be seen that he was not in a happy frame of mind either. Sam was in the glove business and at the moment he was angry because the

Government intended to take the tariff off gloves, or put a tariff on, whichever it was that would hurt him. The three were well acquainted because Sam had married Jesse's sister, Blanche, who had played in the Lasky family band and now designed costumes for a vaudeville producing company Jesse had. Cecil wrote one-act musicals for the company.

As soon as Sam heard about the movie scheme, he said, "I'm in."

That dinner meeting was to have quite an effect on motion picture history, as any moviegoer knows. All three became associates of mine.

Not long after my little verbal excursion into the past, word reached me that the industry was planning to celebrate my eightieth birthday and my fiftieth anniversary in motion pictures. There was to be a banquet in Hollywood, another in New York, others in cities in the United States and abroad. This, I reasoned, happens to a man because he has outlived nearly all of his early associates. Yet when the messages from old friends poured in, and especially after the warm spirit of the banquets, I had to confess that I was moved. And naturally all this carried me back far and deep into the past.

I concluded then that perhaps my memoirs would be of some general interest and of value to historians. They should be, I decided, mainly recollections of the industry. Yet it may be that I will ask forbearance for a degree of sentimentality. After all, I arrived from Hungary an orphan boy of sixteen with a few dollars sewn into my vest. I was thrilled to breathe the fresh strong air of freedom, and America has been good to me.

My wife has been at my side during these celebrations, as she has been during all of my years in the motion picture industry, and many before. To make my story honest I will have to include the heartbreaks too. And I could never have survived these fifty years without the great strength and understanding of my wife.

2

TO put the feature picture and my career in the proper perspective I will need to sketch in what had gone before. Most historians place the beginning of the motion picture industry in 1896, which was seven years before I entered it, on March 3, 1903.

Thomas A. Edison is credited with having made motion pictures possible, though, as in the case of most great inventions, experiments by many others had gone before. In 1891 Edison filed a patent for his Kinetoscope, a peep device. He did not believe that the showing of pictures on a larger screen would be profitable. The Vitascope and the Mutoscope, also peep machines, were put on the market by others.

A coin dropped into a slot allowed the customer to observe about a minute. A typical subject was a cop chasing a tramp, a moving train, perhaps a girl dancing—almost anything which moved rapidly. The peep machines were installed in parlors or arcades along with coin-slot phonographs, the juke boxes of their day.

By 1896 dozens of arcades throughout the country were flourishing, and a few attempts had been made to show the pictures on larger screens. One thing against screen showings was the public's suspicion of a darkened room, especially if a partitioned cubicle in an arcade. Showmen were widely regarded as sly tricksters. People were afraid of being ushered into darkened places and out through a back door without ever seeing a show.

According to a history of the movies I was reading not long ago, the problem was solved by Thomas L. Tally, described as a rough-and-ready ex-cowboy who operated a Los Angeles arcade. He cut peepholes in partition walls to convince prospective customers that movies were actually being shown inside. The idea spread.

That sounds like Tom Tally, for he was a resourceful man, as I can testify. A couple of decades later he was a leader among the film exhibitors who organized the First National company, went into picturemaking, raided me and other producers for stars, and precipitated what has been marked down as one of the titanic struggles of the industry. The action forced me and other producers to lay out, in self-defense, scores of millions of dollars for buying theaters.

Mention of the darkened room caught my attention, for it called to mind one of Sid Grauman's escapades. Nowadays when the story is told, Sam Goldwyn is often substituted as the hero, but it was really Tom Tally. Sid, a bushy-haired, deceptively grave little man, rented a banquet hall, stipulating that it be darkened upon his signal. Then he sent word to Tally that a group of banqueting exhibitors wanted him to address them. Tom was willing to oblige. I don't know how Sid explained the darkness, but he was a convincing talker.

Tom arrived and was soon deep in a ripsnorting oration. No one applauded. Tom roared out his most telling points, and got not so much as a handclap. Being a true showman and old campaigner he took new breath and redoubled his efforts. Finally there was a movement at one of the tables. Tom's eyes were becoming more accustomed to the darkness, and he observed one of the guests topple and fall. He rushed forward, stooped—and picked up a clothing-store dummy.

Now the applause welled up, but it was mingled with laughter and came from Grauman's cronies behind the scenes. He had placed dummies at the first tables and the rest of the room was empty. Tally was cool toward Grauman for a number of years.

But I am getting ahead of early motion picture history. My own first recollection of seeing a film was in Chicago in 1893. Entitled *The Kiss,* it showed May Irwin, one of the famous comediennes of the day, and John C. Rice, a well-known actor, re-enacting the climax of a play in which they had starred. One of May Irwin's comic assets was her very large mouth. While Rice kissed one corner of it, she talked to the audience out of the other. One couldn't hear her, of course, but printed lines were flashed on the screen.

Like the rest of the audience, I enjoyed the picture as

a novelty. But it cannot be reported that a flash of lightning opened the heavens and revealed the future. As a partner in a Chicago fur business, I was, though still under twenty-five, doing quite well and there was no thought in my mind of changing occupations. Concerning the fur business, I will guarantee to provide the reader with all he wants to know about my career in it in a few lines. But it happens that many associates and relatives were to go into motion pictures along with me, and I will hold off until the point where we caught up with the industry. Or, more exactly, the industry caught us up.

Thomas A. Edison stayed in the field, improving and manufacturing mechanical equipment and producing pictures. At West Orange, New Jersey, Edison built the first movie studio, a tiny tar-paper-covered affair nicknamed the Black Maria. Though his company was to remain an industry leader for many years, Edison himself took more interest in the mechanics than the finished product. But I have always believed, as a result of talks with him, that given the time and inclination he would have speeded the development of the film story.

When I came to seek permission of the "trust"—a tight organization of the leading companies—to proceed with feature pictures, I visited Edison at his laboratories. From our conversation it appeared that he seldom viewed motion pictures. But he readily saw the advantages of the feature picture over the one-reeler, after I had outlined them, and used his influence to help me.

Many years later as an honored guest at the opening

of our New York Paramount Theatre, Edison expressed amazement at progress of the film. I gained the impression that he had seen few, if any, pictures since my earlier talk with him. In passing I might note another debt to Edison. During our first visit he pointed to an old horsehair couch in his office and gave me a short lecture on the value of a nap amidst the hardest work or most trying problem. I learned the trick of cutting off one's mind, napping a bit, and waking up with fresh strength to carry on.

It was while working for the Edison company that Edwin S. Porter made his long technical strides in picture-making. Porter was in appearance a rather stolid man, heavy and with a luxuriant mustache, who might have been taken more readily for a brewer than a director, yet he had been a barnstorming showman with the Wormwood Dog and Monkey Show, projecting films in a tent. He had also, more or less fittingly, toured some of the Caribbean countries under the *nom de plume* Thomas A. Edison, Jr., the better to attract audiences. Whether Edison knew about this amiable honor paid him in the hot countries, or would have cared, I do not know. Like all pioneers, Porter was resourceful.

The second of the important early companies was Biograph. The name chiefly associated with it in the beginning was that of W. K. L. Dickson, who had been a laboratory assistant to Edison in the development of his machines. Biograph was well financed, its mechanical equipment was if anything a cut above Edison's, and it got off to a strong start. Had it not begun to fall by the wayside, perhaps the industry would not have had its old lion, Jeremiah J. Kennedy, sent into Biograph by a bank to see about its loans.

Kennedy was a commanding figure come up to wealth through the rough engineering world, and after he became the big boss of the "trust" he roared at all of us who defied him. Hard blows were struck too, and Kennedy was reputed to have a masterful espionage system to ferret out violations of rules he laid down. Kennedy tried to rule the motion picture frontier, but the pioneers were too tough and wily even for him.

The third major company launched before the turn of the century was Vitagraph. It had its inception when J. Stuart Blackton, a young and personable chalk artist, went to West Orange to interview Edison for a New York newspaper. Edison liked Blackton and persuaded him to do chalk portraits of Grover Cleveland and other celebrities before the camera in the Black Maria. In return, Edison allowed Blackton to purchase one of his projection machines, which were in high demand.

Blackton and a young friend of his, Albert E. Smith, who occasionally worked on the same platform as a magician, went into the exhibition business in a small way. After a little they began producing rude pictures of their own, one of which illustrates the movies of the period. As the patriotic fever rose with the outbreak of the Spanish-American War, they mounted a Spanish flag on a pole. While Smith cranked the camera, Blackton snatched the flag down. Only the conquering hand showed. Then an American flag was run up the pole.

The film, titled *Tearing Down the Spanish Flag,* was popular in those vaudeville houses which occasionally ran films between live acts.

Not long afterward, Blackton and Smith took in William "Pop" Rock, a showman in the old tradition. Pop Rock, a big, walrus-mustached man who wore a large gold chain across his vest, owned a New York poolhall but traveled over the land as a showman, lately of pictures. The tri-partnership was formed one night while the three sat on the high stools of Rock's poolroom.

They went on to power and fortune, but Pop Rock remained a colorful showman about whom people liked to tell stories. A favorite was the one in which a company emissary found Pop in a saloon early one morning after a night of regaling himself and the house with liquids. Pop agreed good-naturedly with the emissary that the night was over and tossed a thousand-dollar bill on the bar. The bartender rang up the cash register and handed back a dollar or two.

The emissary was in favor of protesting the accounting.

"No," Pop Rock said, throwing a wise arm around his shoulder, "let us not question matters concerning which we know nothing."

Billy Brady liked to tell how he and Jim Jeffries, a fast man despite his bulk, chased Albert Smith after Smith had made a pirate film of the Jeffries-Tom Sharkey fight. After tearing down the Spanish flag, Blackton and Smith had covered the real war, marching up San Juan Hill with Teddy Roosevelt and Richard Harding Davis. But that experience seems to have been mild compared with Smith's pirating exploit.

Brady had sold the film rights to Biograph, whose crew had rigged up costly lights. Smuggling in a camera, Smith cranked away from a seat a couple of dozen rows from the ringside, happy for rival Biograph's lights. Brady spotted the pirate camera and sent a flying wedge of detectives after it. The excited crowd threw them back. Smith escaped with his film and holed up in a roadhouse. Soon Brady, Jeffries, and assorted attachés located him. There followed a chase which, if filmed, would have rated with the fight picture itself.

Smith eluded his pursuers, developed his film, and took a well-deserved nap in a chair while it dried. By the time Pop Rock appeared and awakened him, a footpad had pirated the pirated film. Spirits were high in those days.

Brady was a jumpy man when it came to prize-fight films, and with some justification. Earlier he had sold rights for the battle between Gentleman Jim Corbett and Ruby Bob Fitzsimmons. Shortly afterward, Sigmund Lubin of Philadelphia, a former novelty peddler and a disciple of Pop Rock, released a film which he described as the Corbett-Fitzsimmons fight "in counterpart." He had hired a couple of muscular roustabouts to re-enact the struggle from press accounts. Lubin went ahead to become a power in the industry.

Another pioneer was Colonel William N. Selig, who had crisscrossed the West with his minstrel show. It was Selig who, on one of these trips, discovered Bert Williams, perhaps the greatest of the Negro comics. The colonel had a flair for spotting talent. Later in Oklahoma he noticed an ex-United States Marshal named Tom Mix lazily watching the filming of a western picture. Selig hoisted Mix into a saddle and turned the camera on him, launching that great film cowboy's career.

Other names which stand out among those starting before the turn of the century are those of George K. Spoor, a news dealer and small showman, and George Kleine, a small tradesman in magic lantern slides. Both operated in Chicago. There were many others. Hundreds, perhaps thousands, took a flyer at the new show business. A few of the stronger and cannier survived.

Most of the films ran only two or three minutes. A perfectly good subject—quite popular, in fact—was a girl climbing an apple tree. Here are a few others taken at random: a tramp stealing a pie, a bad boy lighting a match to his grandfather's newspaper, an elderly businessman caught by his wife in the act of kissing his stenographer, a servant disrupting a swank dinner by spilling food.

The nature of the early movies can probably best be demonstrated by the fact that the first "story" picture was made as late as 1903. It was Edwin S. Porter's *The Great Train Robbery,* which has been recognized, and properly so, as one of the great events of the industry. That is reason enough for including a synopsis here. It should be borne in mind that *The Great Train Robbery,* the most important film of its time, was less than a reel in length, with a showing time of under ten minutes.

Adolph Zukor in his office, Paramount Building, New York (1949).

Adolph Zukor's birthplace in Ricse, Hungary.

Tennis, anyone? Left to right: Marcus Loew, Sam Bernard, Milton Wolff, Lou Teller, and Lew Fields. Zukor is seated on the ground.

1897

1947

Mr. and Mrs. Zukor

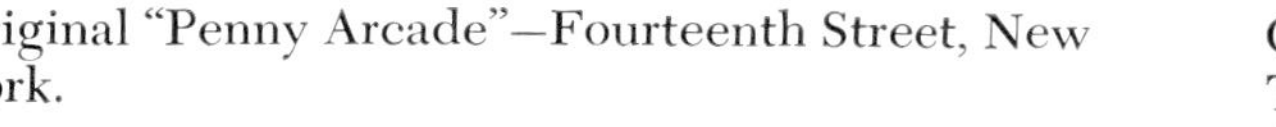

Original "Penny Arcade"—Fourteenth Street, New York.

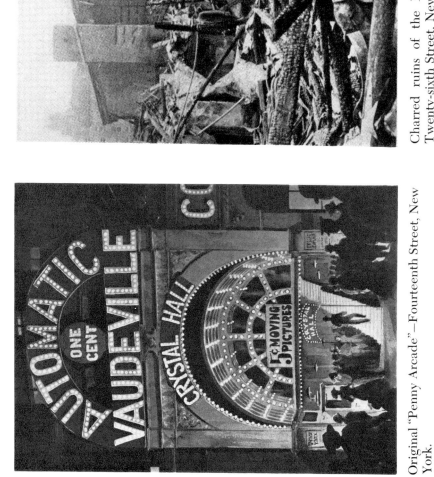

Charred ruins of the Famous Players studio in Twenty-sixth Street, New York. The safe containing the company's film clings to the wall, upper right.

Porter selected a cast, including a stunt man who could fall from a horse, and a vaudeville performer named G. M. Aronson. A story is told that Aronson—who later became G. M. Anderson—had falsely stated he could ride a horse, a fact which is interesting because he was to become Broncho Billy, the first of the cowboy heroes. Porter borrowed a train from the Delaware, Lackawanna, & Western railroad, hired a few horses from a West Orange livery stable, and was ready to go. It is plain that the Edison company had written the production into the budget as an "epic." But it was the skill with which Porter told his story, using flashbacks and careful organization of scenes, which made it a revolutionary film.

The picture begins in a railroad telegraph office, with two masked robbers entering and compelling the operator to signal an approaching train to a halt. They then force him to write a message ordering the engineer to take on water at this station rather than one farther along. The train is seen through the window grinding to a halt. The conductor comes up and takes the message. The bandits, crouched out of sight until the conductor departs, emerge and bind and gag the operator.

The scene shifts to the water tower, behind which two other robbers are hiding. Their comrades from the station join them and all four board the train between the express car and the tender as it pulls out.

Now the camera leaves the robbers and goes inside the express car. The messenger, hearing an unusual sound, peeps through a keyhole and discovers two men trying to break in. Startled, he locks the strong box and throws the key from the train. When the robbers succeed in breaking in, he opens fire and is killed in a pistol duel. The robbers, unable to find the key to the box, blow it open with dynamite.

Now the scene shifts to the other bandits, who have climbed over the tender. One covers the engineer and the other the fireman. But the fireman, grasping his shovel, puts up a fight. A desperate hand-to-hand struggle with one of the bandits follows, with the men in constant danger of falling off the tender. Finally the robber knocks out the fireman with a lump of coal and hurls his body off the train.

The robbers force the engineer to stop, uncouple the engine, and pull it up a hundred feet or so. The passengers are ordered out of the coaches and lined up along the tracks while being searched. One attempts to escape and is instantly shot down.

Boarding the engine, the desperadoes force its driver to take them to a point several miles up the track, where they take to the mountains. Their horses are tethered in a valley. They mount hurriedly and ride into the wilderness.

Now for the revolutionary flashback. In the telegraph office the bound-and-gagged operator struggles to his feet and calls for assistance by manipulating the telegraph key with his chin. Thereupon he faints. His little daughter, entering with his dinner pail, cuts the rope, throws a glass of water into his face, and he rushes out to give the alarm.

All this is done, remember, in a very few moments of film. And so Porter proves himself bold and confident in switching to a totally new scene. It is a western dance hall in which a lively quadrille is being danced. Porter obviously did not want much film to pass through the camera without violent action on it, and a tenderfoot is thrust into the middle of the floor while fun-loving cowboys shoot close to his feet. Suddenly the telegraph operator bursts into the hall. He pants out his message and the men take their rifles and depart.

The next scene shows the mounted robbers hurtling down a rugged hill, hotly pursued by the posse. Both sides fire as they ride. The stunt man, playing one of the desperadoes, plunges headlong from his horse.

Porter had cast well, for the desperado staggered to his feet before being shot dead. Porter couldn't afford to retake scenes like that.

The camera shifts to the three bandits, now dismounted, counting their booty, thinking they have evaded the posse. But the pursuers have dismounted too, and they surround the robbers and open fire. After a desperate battle, all of the robbers and some of the posse "bite the dust," to use the phrase of the Edison catalog of the time.

The film had a capper, or what these days would be called a gimmick or snapperoo. One of the desperadoes appears in a close-up (the catalog called it simply a "life-size picture"), takes careful aim, and fires point-blank at the audience. The Edison company, suggesting to exhibitors that the scene might be used either at the beginning or the end of the film, declared that "the resulting excitement is great."

It generally was, too. For years *The Great Train Robbery* remained a favorite. That desperado, in real life a mild fellow named George Barnes who worked at Huber's Museum on Fourteenth Street, must have fired his pistol at me a thousand times after I got into the exhibition business.

3

NOW, if the reader will bear with me for a few moments, I will get myself into the motion picture business and commence my half century's journey through it.

I was born in a rural Hungarian village called Ricse, where my father had built a small store with his own hands. The store he operated with the help of my mother, for it was necessary also for him to cultivate nearby fields to gain a living for us. I do not, however, remember my father. One day he lifted a heavy box or barrel and broke a vein or vessel in his body. Home remedies failed and finally a doctor was called. Blood poisoning had set in and he soon died.

My mother, who was well educated, being the daughter of a rabbi, was left to fend for my brother Arthur, three years old, and for me, one year old. She was delicate and could not hope to run the store and till the fields. After a little she remarried. Even as a little boy I knew that she had never recovered from the loss of my father. She died when I was eight. My brother and I then lived with a maternal uncle, a rabbi, in a village not far away. My brother was a brilliant student and possessed a wonderful gift of oratory. Our uncle believed that he would some day become a jewel of the church, and he did.

My school marks were not exceptional, and I had no passion for a profession. Consequently, at twelve I was apprenticed for three years to Herman Blau, who had a store in the hamlet of Szanto, a wine-growing center about ten miles from Ricse. My duties were to sweep, run errands, and perform other chores while learning to be a clerk. Two evenings of each week I went to night school.

In Hungary there was little individual freedom or opportunity of rising in life, but an effort was made to look out for orphans. The Government took a part of the estate of the parents and set it aside for the use of the children. Thus, after my father died, a little of the revenue from the store and fields was put into a fund for my brother and me. After my mother died, my step-father was called upon to contribute her share to us.

The store apprenticeship paid nothing beyond board, but twice each year my father's brother, who was trustee of the fund, certified to the Orphans' Bureau my clothing needs. In the spring, around Easter, I would be given a light suit and a pair of shoes. In the fall I would receive a heavier suit, boots, an overcoat if the old one was threadbare, and a few other essentials. None of these clothes were of good quality.

My lot was not a terrible one, for Herman Blau and

his family were kindly people and I did not balk at hard work. But I soon looked about me and was able to see no future. After finishing the apprenticeship I would become a clerk at an equivalent of perhaps two dollars in American money a month, plus board and lodging. Many clerks with whom I was acquainted had worked for a long time for little more. And once a clerk, always a clerk. You might have far better qualifications as a tailor or a carpenter, but to switch from one trade to another was impossible. Even to move from town to town required a certificate from the employer. I could see nothing but darkness in Hungary for me.

All the while, letters were coming to the village from emigrants to America. These, speaking glowingly of freedom and opportunities, were passed from hand to hand. I read them along with such books about America as were available. Whenever someone returned for a visit I was quick with questions about that faraway and promising land. At fourteen I had definitely made up my mind to go. My problem was to figure out how in the world I could make it, for a great deal of money was required to travel to Bremen or Hamburg and take passage on a boat.

My apprenticeship was over in the fall of 1888, when I was fifteen, and I sat down and wrote a letter to the trustee of my orphan's fund. I poured my heart into it, telling of the things I had heard and read of America and begging to be allowed funds to go there.

It made a good impression and I was called before the superintendent of the Orphans' Bureau in a town some distance away. There I poured my heart out again. The superintendent questioned me closely and I could see that he suspected I had done some wrong and wished to escape to America.

He checked up by writing to my boss. But Herman Blau replied that I had done no wrong and he wished me good luck. I had already told him of my ambitions.

The Orphans' Bureau did not give the money directly to me, but to my brother, who was attending the University of Berlin. I was given only a ticket to Berlin and a little money to keep in my pocket for food on the way. After my brother had bought a steamship ticket he made an exchange of the balance into United States money. There was forty dollars and a few pieces of change. We sewed the forty dollars into my vest and he warned me not to take the vest off or touch the money until I had arrived in America.

These instructions I religiously observed, and the vest was still on me when I arrived at Castle Garden, the point at which immigrants then debarked. No sooner did I put my foot on American soil than I was a newborn person. The reader will understand from my background that I am not using an empty phrase in saying that I felt the freedom in the air.

There must have been fifty or more express wagons waiting to take the immigrants to destinations. In my notebook was the address of friends of my parents. On the boat, and long before, I had been trying to learn English. But at Castle Garden no one understood what I said, and I don't blame them.

Finally I showed the address to an expressman and he motioned for me to hoist my suitcase and myself in the wagon. He delivered me to East Second Street for twenty-five cents, which I was able to pay out of the silver in my pocket.

The family had not known that I was coming and did not recognize me. Nevertheless, I was welcomed with open arms. At last my vest and the rest of my clothing came off and I took a bath in a tub in the kitchen. The water running out of the taps did not amaze me, for I was prepared for miracles.

A few days later I was working in an upholstery shop at two dollars a week. Not long afterward I ran into a boy about my own age whom I had known in Hungary. His brother got me a job as an apprentice in a fur shop. I began at a salary of four dollars a week—more than I needed, since board and lodging was only two and a half dollars a week. A kid like myself slept on the sofa in the home of a family whose head earned only ten or twelve dollars a week, and the additional income was welcome.

I was very happy, earning big money, living among hundreds of boys of my own age and interests. We boxed, played baseball, and sang Hungarian songs. Having been to night school in Szanto, it was natural for me to ask right away, "Do you have night school here?" The answer was affirmative and I enrolled.

After learning the fur trade, it occurred to me to go into business for myself. With that thought in mind I went to Chicago, though another reason was that I wanted to see the World's Fair. The shop in which I had worked specialized in fur neckpieces made from a single animal, with the head left on. The style was now catching on in Chicago, and since I knew the methods of preparation there was no trouble finding small contracts to fill. Gradually I went into business for myself.

Each fur scarf had a hook and eye or some other clasp to hold the ends together around the shoulders. I invented a spring that allowed the mouth to open and close, making the mouth itself a clasp. I had never heard of patents, but doubtless a patent would have made little difference, since the method could be changed enough to get by. Nevertheless I was off to a head start and sold my scarves at a good profit.

And so here I was at nineteen, swimming in money. In the next couple of years I accumulated seven or eight thousand dollars, a large sum in those days. Many times I congratulated myself on having composed the letter to my trustee. Even so, I was occasionally homesick, and just before reaching twenty-one I returned for a visit and incidentally saw a number of the sights of Europe.

I gave little thoughts to marriage, except to make a mental note that such an event was unlikely to transpire for many years to come. I did not miss family life, never having had much of it. While not exactly a man about town, I lived well and comfortably in a hotel and often took a girl to the theater or for dining and dancing.

I was to learn that it is one thing to plan bachelorhood, another to carry out the plan.

One dealer in raw furs with whom I did business was Morris Kohn, a fellow Hungarian some ten years older than myself. He had entered the fur trade in a rather curious way. With his sister and brother-in-law, Mr. and Mrs. Herman Kaufman, he had taken up homesteading in the Devil's Lake section of North Dakota. To supplement the farm income, Morris had traded with the Sioux Indians for raw pelts. In that way he learned about furs, and after returning to Chicago he stayed in the business.

The Kaufmans had stayed on for a few years in their sod house, but finally they too returned to Chicago, partly because the region was thinly settled and they wanted their daughters to have a chance to meet eligible men.

One Sunday afternoon I called at Morris Kohn's home to keep a business appointment. When the maid told me he had not yet returned from a drive with a niece, I seized the opportunity to join a game of baseball in a vacant lot nearby. A broken finger which remained stiff had finished me as a catcher, and now I valued myself as a second baseman. I am told that it was while I was fielding a grounder—without an error, I hope—that my future wife laid eyes on me for the first time.

Morris Kohn had returned with his niece Lottie Kaufman, second of the four daughters of that pioneer North Dakota sod house. Lottie was unimpressed by my baseball skill, or, at first, by me. But I was not long acquainted with the slender Lottie, with her beautiful dark eyes and exquisite skin, before my notions about marriage began to change.

The courtship was nevertheless rather slow in getting under way. There were many suitors and I was required to play a vast number of hands of cards at the homes of Morris Kohn and Herman Kaufman before my presence was felt. Gradually Lottie and I became better acquainted. She had been born in Hungary too, in a rural area like my own. She was quiet, yet full of warm laughter, and very discerning—a natural homemaker. We were married on January 10, 1897, a week after my twenty-fourth birthday.

About this time Morris Kohn and I went into partnership as Kohn & Company, manufacturing furriers. Morris was a genial man, easy to meet, with a wide acquaintanceship in the trade, and at first he handled most of the outside business. It was while on the road that he first met Marcus Loew, then also a furrier, a dandy in a high hat and fur-lined coat. Marcus was a retiring fellow but he said the high hat and coat impressed the trade. The showman was there all the time. After Kohn & Company moved to New York, in 1900, we lived across from the Loews at 111th Street and Seventh Avenue and were soon warm friends.

It was two years later that I first began to think about going into the motion picture business, or a phase of it. This was before the term Nickelodeon had been invented. In Los Angeles, Tom Tally had converted his arcade into The Electric Theater, "For Up-to-Date Motion Picture Entertainment Especially for Ladies and

Children." But the peep machines were still the main outlets for such films as were being made.

My first interest in the show business came through the conversation of a cousin, Max Goldstein, an importer, who had gone to the Exposition in Buffalo to introduce Puerto Rican cigars. While there he had become acquainted with Mitchell Mark and a friend of his named Wagner, who were operating a penny arcade at the Exposition. Mitchell Mark was to make a large name for himself with construction of the Strand Theater on Broadway, the first of the big houses devoted exclusively to pictures. And he was a founder along with Tom Tally and other exhibitors of First National.

Mark and Wagner came down to New York and with Max Goldstein opened a small arcade on 125th Street. Out of curiosity, Morris Kohn and I accompanied Max on a visit to it. We peeped into the movie machines and listened to the phonographs—which were still the main part of the business—and stood about observing the interest of the customers. This was my first experience in studying audiences, and I have been doing it ever since. After becoming more interested in the operation, I studied the "box-office" figures, another vital thing to do.

At that time the center of show business in New York was Fourteenth Street. In time the conversation got around to the possibilities of a penny arcade in that section. Such a venture would cost a lot of money. It would require a certain amount of glamor, the rent would be high, and expensive kinetoscope and phonograph machines and special cabinets would have to be purchased from Edison. The total cost, the three partners estimated, would run to $75,000—a sum far beyond their reach.

After a dozen conferences and much figuring, Morris Kohn and I agreed to provide the necessary cash and credit. Neither of us expected to leave the fur trade, but it was agreed that one ought to spend a reasonably large share of his time keeping an eye on the arcade, especially since Mark and Wagner remained in Buffalo and Goldstein continued with his import business. The assignment went first to Kohn.

We leased a building on East Fourteenth Street at Broadway, where Ohrbach's department store now stands. A restaurant occupied the first floor, which ran through to Thirteenth Street. It was ripped out and the long room redecorated with bright colors and flashing lights. A hundred or more peep machines were installed, about 60 per cent of them phonographs and the rest motion pictures. The phonographs were the more popular because changes of records were available. Sufficient film was hard to get.

Other slot machines delivered peanuts, candy, and the like. Everything cost a penny, a penny to get in and a penny a look, a listen, or a handful of food. Morris Kohn, in an inventive turn of mind, rigged up a small locomotive which ran around a track and released the coins into itself.

The basement contained a shooting gallery and various athletic devices—punching bags, stationary bicycles, hobbyhorses. Everything was a penny here too, including the shooting. The gallery was operated something like the electric-eye galleries of today. One dropped a penny in a slot, aimed a gun, and pulled the trigger. I don't know the exact science of it, but somehow the target registered the hit.

From the beginning the enterprise was a success, the daily take ranging from five hundred to seven hundred dollars. Our fur offices were nearby on Twelfth Street, and, though handling the main end there, I couldn't keep away from the arcade.

By the end of 1903 we were expanding to Newark, Philadelphia, and Boston, with the result that Kohn and I decided to close out our fur business to devote full energies to the arcades. The liquidation was time consuming, and, since neither of us wanted to be tied down, we brought in Emil Shauer, a buyer for Mandel Brothers' store in Chicago and a brother-in-law of Kohn's, as manager of the arcades.

Marcus Loew, hearing us talk about the arcades, wanted in. So did David Warfield. We could make only a little room for them, since the enterprise was already crowded with partners. But Loew got his feet wet and soon began looking for a place to open an arcade of his own.

Our next step was to convert the floor over the Fourteenth Street Arcade to a motion picture theater. Workmen ripped and hammered, and in 1904 the Crystal Hall, as we named the theater, was ready. To reach it, Morris had devised a glass staircase; inside it water cascaded over lights of changing colors.

While not the first theater devoted to motion pictures, it was perhaps the most attractive of its time.

4

MY first experience in watching audiences was, as I have said, at the little arcade while Morris Kohn and I were deciding whether to invest money in a bigger one. I had continued to watch them at the Fourteenth Street Arcade. There wasn't, of course, much that could be learned from peepers, since the shows themselves were hardly anything to base judgment on. We kept a "box office" on the machines, but it proved little except that the public wanted action, romance, and comedy.

Crystal Hall patrons got a fifteen-minute show for a nickel. There were usually three little subjects along the lines I indicated, though some better material was arriving from France. The works of Georges Méliès were remarkable for their time. Having been a magician, he developed camera tricks which gave many of his pictures a fairy-tale quality, and his *Cinderella* was a popular feature.

I admired Méliès and some years later tried to search him out in France, but this early genius had dropped mysteriously out of sight, to come to public attention decades later when discovered selling newspapers on the Paris streets. But I was to know another French giant, Charles Pathé, at whose estate and studios I spent many pleasant and instructive hours discussing the future of motion pictures.

In the Crystal Hall it was my custom to take a seat about six rows from the front. Numerous patrons stayed through more than one show, but those departing from my neighborhood doubtless regarded me as a fellow with the least to do of anybody in New York. Probably they had already concluded that my mind wandered, for I spent a good deal of time watching the faces of the audience, even turning around to do so.

A movie audience is very sensitive. With a little experience I could see, hear, and "feel" the reaction to each melodrama and comedy. Boredom was registered —even without comments or groans—as clearly as laughter demonstrated pleasure.

Let me take this opportunity to reassure patrons of the Paramount Theatre in New York who have been, or may yet be, mildly perturbed by an elderly neighbor who seems to have bought a seat only for a chance to sit down. By now, it is true, I am a sly audience watcher, and of course I wait until the film is on before starting my peeping. I need not more than glance at the picture, for I will have seen it in the projection room before going from my ninth-floor office down to the theater.

But in a projection room no one, however much his

experience, can judge an audience's reaction—and it is surprising how wrong one can be. Generally by the time we executives in New York gauge the audience feeling, the director and the producer and perhaps some of the actors have had their moments of terror at the sneak previews, and have made some changes. From our audience observations we make decisions on the best ways of promotion, how much to spend, and the like. Or we may send the film back to Hollywood for improvement.

Day after day we follow and try to anticipate the public's desires. Films of rival companies are shown in our projection rooms. But I feel out of touch unless I pay my money at box offices as I walk about the city and watch pictures with the audiences.

Half a century ago, sitting on a hard chair in Crystal Hall, I felt the impact of Porter's *The Great Train Robbery*. But we couldn't run it every day, and the Edison company was simply having Porter grind out imitations of his masterpiece. The other companies flattered him with emulation too. Otherwise there were no major changes.

Nevertheless I was convinced that motion pictures had a bright future. Near the Fourteenth Street Arcade was an available store building which I favored converting into a street-level movie house. My partners held that a new theater would hurt the Crystal Hall trade, not realizing that movie theaters might be grouped, as they are in Times Square today. I took the lease in my own name but did nothing about conversion immediately.

I was finding the show business very much to my liking. Those of us who became film producers hailed from all sorts of occupations—furriers, magicians, butchers, boilermakers—and for this reason highbrows have sometimes poked fun at us. Yet one thing is certain—every man who succeeded was a born showman. And once in the show business he was never happy out of it. Motion picture production has always been a hazardous and highly competitive enterprise. It was common for a showman to be forced to the wall, knocked down, jumped on. And next day he would appear, like an India-rubber man, in the same shape and as if nothing had happened. Myself too, I am proud to say.

I recall my pleasure in securing a wax fortunetelling gypsy lady in Europe for the Fourteenth Street Arcade. This lady, whom we called Esmeralda, was responsible for a story that I augmented my income by writing the text for the fortunetelling slips of the kind which are found in penny scales and the almond cookies served in Chinese restaurants. The tale was repeated by Cecil De Mille at the Hollywood banquet marking my eightieth birthday. And, being a deft hand with a story, before Cecil was through he had me still rushing to a Chinese bakery every morning with a fresh batch of fortunes. There is a slight basis for this legend.

In Europe—I think in Zurich—I saw in a doctor's office a number of wax limbs which had been constructed by a workman whose shop was in the mountains. The idea of a wax gypsy woman occurred to me. This man had never, it turned out after I reached his shop, made mechanical figures. But after giving some thought to the matter he decided that he could make a gypsy woman who would, when a penny was dropped in a slot, turn and pick a slip of paper out of a bowl. He did a beautiful job. In a gypsy dress and shawl she looked quite lifelike sitting in her glass case.

The gypsy was a hit at the arcade, dropping her little fortunes through a chute. Emil Shauer, the arcade manager, enjoyed writing those fortunes. He was a cultured man, widely traveled, and eventually he was to set up our picture business abroad. But he liked nothing better than to write those fortunes. His wife Julie, one of the Kaufman sisters, was telling me only recently that he used to wake her up in the middle of the night to get her opinion of a new gem he had polished.

Many years later, after our picture business had grown large, a Chinaman came into our main New York offices with one of those old gypsy slips which carried on the back the arcade's name and a copyright. Somehow he had traced it all the way to us, and he wanted others to put into almond cookies. I happened to pass by the receptionist's desk and sent him in to see Emil Shauer, who was the company's treasurer. Emil received the Chinaman courteously and told him yes, the slogan was his handiwork, but he had gotten out of the fortune-writing business. He dug up the name of a novelty company which produced such things and the Chinaman thanked him and departed.

When I went into Emil's office a while later he was sitting at his desk staring into space. Under my cross-examination he admitted that a couple of slogans had struck him. I think he was sorry to have let the Chinaman get away.

Not long ago, while walking on Sixth Avenue in New York, I was brought up short. There, staring at me, was Esmeralda. She sat, rather the worse for wear, in her glass case at the entrance to an arcade. The mechanism had been changed, and I was required to drop in two pennies before she was ready to address me, as follows:

> The devil and his pitch fork are gadding about
> The devil will get you if you don't watch out.
> He places temptation in your way.
> Be strong, be firm and you won't stray.

I tipped my hat and passed on, feeling that Emil Shauer would have wanted to do a bit of polishing before letting the verse go to the printer.

I am jumping ahead again, and will return to that empty store I had leased. As a sideline, William A. Brady had bought the New York rights to the Hale's Tours, developed by George C. Hale, ex-chief of the Kansas City fire department. The tours had been popular at the St. Louis Exposition in 1903.

Hale had built a motion picture theater in the shape of a typical railroad coach of the day. The ticket-collector was dressed as a conductor and the show was advertised as "Hale's Tours of Scenes of the World." A whistle tooted, a bell clanged, the train rocked, and motion pictures of mountains, canyons, waving trees, and the like were thrown on the screen. Audiences really got a sensation of traveling. Many of the pictures had been taken from the rear platforms of moving trains.

When first viewing Cinerama many decades later, I mystified my companions by laughing. It was necessary to explain that I was back in Hale's Tours.

Billy Brady, as his friends called him, looked over possible sites on Fourteenth Street, was impressed with the above-mentioned store, and of course had to come to me about the lease. We had several conversations. I was reluctant to give up the site. And of course the tours were a small item in Brady's enterprises. The logical thing was to pool these small portions of our resources, and we did. I would run the business and report from time to time to Brady. If we made money, that was fine. At any rate, I would learn more about theater operation.

At first the Hale's Tours were a great success. We established others in Pittsburgh, Newark, Coney Island, and perhaps another place or two that I have forgotten.

Then they flopped. The reason was simple. We could not change the films often enough to bring patrons back. We searched the market and failed to discover enough of the special type we required. Suddenly we were losing money.

Brady favored closing up. But I thought I knew more about the picture business than he did because of my time sitting with audiences and talking with members as they departed. Brady had never done that. Though as fine a man as there came, at this stage of his career he would not have wanted to be caught dead by any of his friends in a movie house.

I suggested that we convert to straight moving pictures, throwing out the railway props. I made a test, using *The Great Train Robbery*. As the "train" reached the summit of Mount Blanc or the head of the Royal Gorge, I had it grind to a halt. Then the robbery film was thrown on the screen. The audience interest picked up.

Brady agreed to go ahead, as long as his name was not openly attached to the project.

By this time the term Nickelodeon had come in. It was invented, I understand, by John P. Harris and Harry Davis for their little store theater in Pittsburgh. They combined "nickel" and "*odeon*," the Greek word for theater. The happy choice caught on, sometimes changed to "Nicolet" or "Nickelet." The big sweep was in 1905-6 and of course our five-cent Crystal Hall had been ahead of it. But there is no doubt that the term Nickelodeon was an important though temporary factor in the growth of the film industry.

Nevertheless, we passed the term by and called our new venture the Comedy Theater. Nickelodeon would not have fitted since we charged a dime. Despite the "Comedy" in the title, *The Great Train Robbery* remained a chief standby. Business picked up—for a while.

Marcus Loew had gone into the penny-arcade business on his own, but with the rise of Nickelodeons had switched to motion pictures. William Fox did about the same thing. I notice that movie historians refer to Fox as a former "pants sponger," and maybe he was. But he was an entertainer too. As one of a team billed as the Schmaltz Brothers he had enjoyed a minor success in the neighborhood of Fourteenth Street. Fox set up a film exchange, a fact which was to prove important to the industry a few years later.

Unhappily, the public began to lose interest in films about 1907-8. The novelty had worn off and the picture-makers remained in a rut. There were attacks, too, from ministers and reformers. Even *The Great Train Robbery* was a blood-and-thunder thriller and consequently was lumped with the dime novels. We avoided salacious pictures, yet many were being made and shown widely.

Marcus Loew lost faith in the movies and switched almost entirely to vaudeville. Other houses did the same. Now the motion picture became known as a "chaser," a boring device to drive patrons from a vaudeville house to make room for others. We, too, switched to vaudeville, though not to the extent that Loew did. I remember particularly a slender, supple girl named Sophie Tucker who did blackface songs for us.

About this time I went into talking pictures. Edison and others were working on mechanical devices with some success. One might say I was like the old treadmill operators who used human power instead of machines. I simply put live actors behind the screen. One of them,

I recall, was Lowell Sherman, who later became a Broadway star.

A writer was employed to study the films and prepare scripts for the actors, trying to synchronize dialogue with the action. The players—five or six of them—took their cues from watching the pictures in reverse on the back of the screen. The scheme was popular enough that the Keith circuit booked it as a headliner throughout the country.

That lasted a couple of years and died out for the same reason that Hale's Tours did. We ran out of subjects which lent themselves to dialogue. There were no pictures made especially for the purpose and the moment the available subjects were used up our "talkies" were dead.

By now Marcus Loew was expanding rapidly and I was working closely with him. In fact, when he consolidated his enterprises I became treasurer of the company. Yet we were not corporate figures sitting aloft counting our profits. We toured the city by day and by night and, as I have said, met at Shanley's for a late dinner along with Brady, the Shuberts, the Schencks, and others.

Even my children, Mildred and Eugene, did chores about the theaters. One of their tasks was to go along the rows folding the seats. Mildred tells me that to this day, though in evening clothes at a first night, she instinctively folds up the seats in her row as she leaves.

To manage the Comedy Theater I brought in Al Kaufman, my wife's brother, who had come on from Chicago. He was to play an important part in the rise of feature pictures. Though born in the Kaufman pioneer sod house, Al at twenty did not look as if he would be at home behind a plow. He was slight and extremely dapper, carrying a cane and wearing a pearl-gray hat and matching spats. He had enjoyed working as a Coney Island barker prior to coming in as manager.

Al was a fellow who had a dozen adventures every day, some of them fantastic, and none planned. Things happened to Al. Later in Hollywood he became a bosom crony of the celebrated wit Wilson Mizner, of Mack Sennett, and of the great clowns of the Keystone Comedies. I would hesitate to believe in Damon Runyon's characters had I not seen those who flocked around Al.

The Comedy was not an exclusive theater. In fact, the ushers carried blackjacks. Al was mildly surprised when a couple of his regular patrons were arrested for the murder of Herman Rosenthal the gambler. These were Gyp the Blood and Lefty Louie, who had occasionally left their girl friends under Al's eye while they went about their businesss.

One of Al's favorites was a tough character named Dutch Mack. Al and Dutch became acquainted in a somewhat curious fashion. Soon after Al's inauguration as manager, Dutch dropped in and explained that he and his pals expected to see the picture without paying. Without hesitation Al hauled off and hit Dutch Mack as hard as he could. It was a lucky punch, for Dutch went down, and the ushers threw him out.

Later a couple of rough-looking gentlemen came in and approached Al, who signaled to his forces. But the gentlemen were in a pleasant frame of mind. They identified Dutch Mack, remarking that he could put a thumb on Al's head and grind him through the floor. But Dutch had admired Al's spunk. In a little while he came in too, and, after becoming better acquainted the group, offered Al protection against any other gate crashers.

Al was in the box office one evening when a little girl with long golden curls came up to buy a ticket.

"How old are you?" Al asked. The law forbade admittance of a child under sixteen unless accompanied by an adult.

"Sixteen," the girl answered.

"Go get your mother," Al said. "You don't look sixteen."

The girl flared up. "Now, see here! I'm sixteen and besides you're showing my picture inside this minute." She pointed to one of the crude yellow posters which bore her likeness. "I'm working at the Biograph studios up the street and they send the films out in such a hurry I never see my own. And I intend to see one right now."

Al shrugged. "I know you're in the picture," he said. "And I don't care if you're Miss Biograph, you can't come in here without an older person because I think you're under sixteen. The cops will close us up."

Mary Pickford stayed angry about that incident, and when she next saw Al, some years later, she tackled him on it. Al was actually a fan, as was I, of the girl Biograph identified only as "Little Mary." Her picture was on the wall of our little Comedy office, which was reached by a ladder.

Years later in Hollywood, during my absences, the tempestuous Mary would not allow anybody from the business office to come on the lot except Al.

5

MY faith in motion pictures was increasing despite the fact that the current producers seemed bent on killing them. The "trust" was reaching for a strangle hold, beginning in 1910 with the Patents Company and following with the General Film Company. The name of the first told much of the story. The companies in it were largely interested in selling mechanical equipment to theaters. The General Film Company, made up of the same firms, licensed theaters and distributed film.

The moment an "outlaw" piece of equipment or film appeared in a movie house, the license was withdrawn and the supply of "trust" pictures cut off. As an additional weapon, the "trust" contracted with the Eastman Kodak Company, major supplier of raw film, to sell stock only to licensed companies.

The companies involved were Edison, Biograph, Vitagraph, Essanay, Kalem, Selig, George Kleine, and the American branches of Pathé and Méliès. The name Essanay was derived from the initials of the last names of

George K. Spoor and G. M. Anderson. By now Anderson was launched on his career as Broncho Billy, hero of hundreds of western one-reelers. The term Kalem arose from the initials of George Kleine, Samuel Long, and Frank Merriam. Kleine also owned exchanges, which accounted for his two places in the "trust."

There was opposition. William Fox refused to sell his New York film exchange and went to court with an anti-trust suit. The major producer fighting the "trust" was Carl Laemmle, with his Independent Motion Picture Company, usually called IMP. He followed with Universal, in association with Charles O. Bauman and Adam Kessel. Other strong independents were John R. Frueler and Harry E. Aitken with their Mutual Film Corporation. Smaller independents battled on the fringes.

These were hectic days, for J. J. Kennedy—often called Fighting Jeremiah—was not a man to trifle with. As head of the "trust," he sent his process servers, and sometimes servers without processes, against the "outlaws." History is not absolutely clear on the point, but it appears that southern California was first "discovered" for movies by small producers who wanted to be able to skip across the Mexican border at a moment's notice.

The independents kept going, but their point of view on the subject matter of pictures was as narrow as that of the old companies. D. W. Griffith, it is true, was making technical strides at Biograph. A tall, hawk-faced Kentuckian, he had been a reporter and stock actor before drifting shamefacedly into films as an actor and script writer. Even after becoming a director, in 1908, he called himself Lawrence Griffith, reserving "David Wark" until he reached fame. This, he thought, was to be as a writer of books.

Early camera technique was to photograph a scene from a distance, as if all the actors were on a stage. Griffith was the first to bring the camera close to a single actor. The result, known as a full shot, was the forerunner of the close-up. He moved the camera far back for long shots. The dream balloon was in use, but Griffith boldly switched to the object of an actor's thoughts. The fade-out is credited to him also.

But Griffith was feeling his way and besides was hamstrung by the standpat notions of his employers. When Griffith made a two-reel picture, it was released in two parts. The common feeling was that a picture of more than ten to twelve minutes' running time would not hold an audience's attention.

I disagreed. Amidst derision at the dinner table at Shanley's I argued that people would sit through a good story even if it ran an hour or longer.

The feature picture was not, of course, an original idea, being simply a parallel of the average stage play. The Europeans were making a few multireel pictures. But when they arrived in the United States the "trust" broke them down to single reels for release. The truth was that, although twelve thousand to fifteen thousand theaters showed pictures at least part of the time, the "flickers" were widely regarded as a fad which would decline, if not disappear.

I decided to put my theories to a test. The best film

Sarah Bernhardt as Queen Elizabeth (1912).

Jesse Lasky, Adolph Zukor, Sam Goldwyn, Cecil B. De Mille, and Al Kaufman (about 1916).

At banquet honoring Mr. Zukor's 50 years in the motion picture industry (1953)—Mr. Goldwyn, Mr. De Mille, Mr. Lasky, Mr. Zukor.

Mary Pickford in *Poor Little Rich Girl* (1917).

Douglas Fairbanks and Mary Pickford with Adolphe Menjou in *The Taming of the Shrew* (1929).

Marguerite Clark

Rudolph Valentino and Adolphe Menjou

available was a three-reel version of the *Passion Play* which had been made in Europe. I purchased, at a rather high fee, the right to show it. The nature of the film presented certain problems. Religious subjects had been shown in the past with success, but now many churchmen were denouncing motion pictures in general for lack of morality. Some even maintained that movie houses were an invitation to license because of the darkness.

For the test I chose our small theater in Newark, which was located where the Bamberger Department Store now stands. If protests were made against the film as sacrilegious, or the audiences refused to sit through it (running time was about forty-five minutes), I did not expect to try it in New York. An organ was installed and an experienced church organist hired. The posters for the front of the little store theater were dignified and well printed.

Bright and early on the morning of the opening I was in Newark. In those days we opened early and ran late, grinding out film as long as people would come. I stood outside and watched the women come downtown to shop. They looked at the posters with interest, and they listened to the religious music from the organ. Some were drawn inside.

I followed as soon as the show started. The scene was one of the most remarkable I have ever witnessed. Many women viewed the picture with religious awe. Some fell to their knees. I was struck by the moral potentialities of the screen.

At the same time, the excess of emotions indicated the magnitude of the disaster that might overtake my venture.

I returned to the street to wait, knowing that a representative of one or more of the churches would appear. By this time the film had played over once or twice, and of course the posters had gone up the night before. A single objection was sure to close the play. The loss of money would be far less important to me than loss of the opportunity to test my audience theories.

Around eleven o'clock an elderly priest approached. I stepped forward and welcomed him to the play. Before he went in, however, I begged a few moments to explain that it was deeply religious in tone and for many had been a truly religious experience. I did remark, in passing, that were he to put in a complaint the play would surely be closed.

After listening in silence, the priest entered and viewed the picture. When he came out he shook hands, thanked me, and left without comment. The next hours were full of anxiety.

But no summons came that day or any other. The *Passion Play* had a good run in Newark and afterwards at our other theaters. It satisfied me that feature pictures would be successful even though my colleagues were as skeptical as ever.

Recently in my library I ran across a volume titled *The Theatre of Science* by Robert Grau, published in 1914, which describes me as having "the face and eyes of a dreamer." Whether Grau, a well-known theatrical figure of his day, was entirely apt, I feel that he was nearer the mark than later historians who spoke of me as cold. Grau had occasionally listened to me hold forth on that subject. His reproduction is overformal, but I will borrow a quotation.

"Think of what we would have today if moving pictures had been invented five hundred years ago," Grau quoted me as saying. "Consider how history would have been enriched, how facilities of education would have been improved. Think how intimately all the great figures in stage history—Shakespeare, David Garrick, Kemble, Macready, Edwin Forrest, Rachel—would be revealed to us. The light of their genius would be imperishable and shine as brightly for us today as it did in the heyday of their glorious careers. What a difference that would make to humanity. If we can give future generations what we of the present have missed, I shall be more than satisfied."

Use of such flowery language would have caused a bad evening for me at Shanley's, with master ribbers like Marcus Loew and Sam Bernard at hand. Yet this was the way my mind was working, and one night I hit upon a name which expressed my ideas. It came to me while I was riding home on the subway. My brain was tired and consequently I jotted it down on the back of an envelope. Trouble was that next morning I couldn't read my handwriting.

Later, after mental jogging and study, I was able to make it out. The name was "Famous Players in Famous Plays."

To bring this to reality was plainly a big order for an operator of small picture theaters and vaudeville houses. With my interest in various projects, including the Loew firm, I was worth three or four hundred thousand dollars. Loew depended on cheap vaudeville acts, leaving the higher paid to the Keith circuit. When it is remembered that even third-rate stage actors then had extreme contempt for the "flickers," it can readily be seen that I was not in a strong position to approach the stars or great producers. There was need for a man with influence in the theatrical world.

My thoughts turned naturally to Billy Brady. One day I broached the subject to him while we were having lunch together. Before I had gone far, he stopped me gently.

"Adolph," Billy said, "I'll tell you a secret. Before my wife agreed to marry me I had to promise to quit promoting prize fights. Now, if I have given up prize fights, how in the world do you expect me to go into motion-picture making?"

That was that. A few years later when Brady entered movie production he had missed his golden opportunity.

Then a chance arrived to try out my theories on a fairly large scale. One day Carl Laemmle brought Edwin S. Porter to the Comedy Theater to see me. I was well acquainted with Laemmle, whose life had much in common with mine. He had landed in New York alone from Germany at seventeen with fifty dollars in his pocket. For the next twenty years he had worked at small salaries in an Oshkosh, Wisconsin, clothing store. Then on

Chicago's west side in 1906 he opened a little nickel theater and his rise was swift.

They called him "Lucky" Laemmle, which was not especially apt even though he used it himself. He was a tiny man full of fight and he moved like a whirlwind, never sending a letter when a telegram would do as well. I had tried to sell him on feature pictures without success.

Porter, stolid, smoking a big cigar, told me that he had left Edison to form his own company, the Rex. We talked of a number of things that day, but what caught my attention was Porter's mention of the fact that Louis Mercanton, a French producer, wanted to make a four-reel picture with the world-famous Sarah Bernhardt in her successful play *Queen Elizabeth.* Although nearly seventy, the great actress was playing regularly, chiefly in France, her homeland.

Porter told me that Mercanton was being delayed for lack of money. I was elated by Porter's information. First of all, I was a devoted admirer of Sarah Bernhardt and saw her perform every chance I got. An opportunity to help bring her to the screen would delight me. And here might be a real test of my views on feature pictures.

After Porter and Laemmle departed I did some hard thinking. Next day I got in touch with Mercanton's American agent. We discussed the possibility of securing the North American rights. In the end I agreed to pay forty thousand dollars for them, advancing the money to enable Mercanton to go ahead.

It was a long gamble. But I decided that, while waiting

for *Queen Elizabeth,* I would take a further risk by producing feature pictures in America.

Marcus Loew, when he heard of my decisions, felt duty bound as an old friend of the family to warn my wife that I had lost my head and that he expected my money to follow it soon.

6

MARCUS LOEW was doubly worried because I planned to sell part of my stock in the company which bore his name and step out as treasurer. Not that my departure was serious, for he had a fine general manager in Nick Schenck, an excellent talent man in Joe Schenck, and other good executives. He knew that I was selling my stock because it was the only way I had to raise money. All movie men were looked on askance when they walked into a bank. Little consideration would be given to an untried producer with a scheme regarded in the industry itself as crazy.

My wife brought up Loew's warning, not in panic, but to let me know how upset Marcus really was. The feature picture idea was known to her from endless discussions. My work often kept me out late, but the atmosphere of our house was always warm and intimate. My children tell me that even as teen-agers they expressed their film ideas and I listened. Doubtless I did this as a father. Yet they were moviegoers, discussed the pictures with other children, and consequently their audience reactions were of value.

I reassured my wife by pointing out that Marcus was interested chiefly in the business end of the theaters. He was always looking around for new properties and better ways of management. Also, he relied chiefly on vaudeville at the box office. He did not pay much attention to pictures or watch picture audiences.

"I know pretty much what I am doing," I told my wife. "It's a risk, but the stakes are high, and I am calculating the risk."

That was enough for her. If she worried, and of course there were times when she did, her concern was never added to mine. When events weighed heavily on me, she knew how to ease them. At a low point she might arrange—unbeknown to me—to move to cheaper living quarters. In later years she would go into the kitchen, no matter how many cooks, butlers, and the like were about, and prepare some Hungarian dish which she knew would cheer me.

In trying to launch feature pictures my major problem, aside from money, continued to be the finding of a theatrical figure who could break down the barriers between the stage and screen. One day I discussed the matter with my lawyer Elek Ludvigh. He thought over the matter, stroking the goatee he always wore, and remarked that he was a relative of the Frohmans, Daniel and Charles, who were among the great theatrical producers, operating separately. He offered to find out if either was interested enough to discuss the matter with me.

After a few days he brought back word that Charles, the younger and larger operator of the two, had received the suggestion coldly. Daniel, on the other hand, had expressed a mild interest and had agreed to a conversation.

Naturally I jumped at the chance to talk with him. Our appointment was in his studio and living quarters over the Lyceum Theatre. He had turned sixty, but his tall figure was straight, and his goatee and pince-nez gave him a cultivated, aristocratic air. Of the old school, he wore a very high stock collar and, when outdoors, a large soft hat.

The meeting was at night, and after a cordial greeting he guided me to a small trap door which looked down upon the stage. He had been watching a play which was in progress. I cannot recall the title at the moment, but after we had observed for a little while he closed the door and we settled into the easy chairs.

The studio—he called it his sanctuary—was filled with mementos of his long and illustrious career. There was a big throne chair which had been used in a starring vehicle of James K. Hackett, the matinee idol. On the walls were inscribed photographs of Lily Langtry, Minnie Maddern Fiske, E. H. Sothern, Forbes-Robertson, Joseph Jefferson, and many other stage luminaries. Naturally I had a feeling of exhilaration, for here was an atmosphere of famous players in famous plays.

"My brother Charles tells me," Daniel Frohman said, leaning back, relaxed, "that transferring plays to the screen is a ridiculous and quixotic dream. I'm not sure that I agree with him."

I opened with my heaviest gun. "Sarah Bernhardt is not a ridiculous figure. In Paris even now she is being photographed in *Queen Elizabeth.*"

Frohman nodded. "So I have heard. She has remarked that the film offers her a chance for immortality. I think the Divine Sarah has already gained it, but, as you say, no one can speak of her as ridiculous. Is Lou Tellegen playing the Earl of Essex?"

"Yes," I said. "Her whole company is playing."

"And Elek Ludvigh tells me that you will show *Queen Elizabeth* in this country?"

I answered that my intention was to show it, and more. I outlined my plan to charge a higher rental, which I believed that exhibitors would pay once they realized the box-office potentials. With *Queen Elizabeth* I expected to prove that the feature picture could be a success in America.

"But," I went on, "I want to follow at once with feature films made here. I need help in securing the plays and the players—the reason, as you know, for my presence here."

Frohman gestured toward the throne chair. "Now, James K. Hackett, who used that chair in one of my productions, is a fellow not easily deterred by criticism. He wouldn't be worried by what other stage people say. And he often needs money. I have no idea whether he would be interested. But what could you pay him, or someone of his stature?"

I answered without hesitation. "Twice as much as he makes on the stage. Whatever his weekly salary, I'll double it for the time the film is in production."

Frohman nodded as though impressed. "The medium is so different, and the players would worry about that. They depend on their voices which on the screen would be useless. Would you provide stage directors whom they trust?"

"No," I answered. "Because the stage director would be lost at the beginning as much as the actors. I want either D. W. Griffith or Edwin S. Porter, the best of the screen directors. Knowing the camera technique, they will help the players adjust to it."

Much more was said, of course, but the above gives an idea of the trend of the conversation. Frohman made no commitments. But I have always placed that night as one of the most important in the history of motion pictures. Thereafter Frohman was a powerful advocate of the movies in the theatrical world. He traveled extensively in it as well as in society. Everywhere he went he lent his prestige and eloquence to the films.

It was said that Daniel Frohman joined me, as he subsequently did, because he was strapped for money. That was not the case. He simply became convinced of the bright future of motion pictures and had the courage of his convictions.

My next move was to talk with D. W. Griffith. In years past I had visited the Biograph studios in a brownstone house on Fourteenth Street, where I had met him. It had been little more than a shaking of hands, because my plans were only germinating in my mind.

Over a dinner at Luchow's Restaurant on Fourteenth Street, famous then as today, we talked about the possibilities of feature pictures. Griffith believed in them. All serious directors saw in them a greater opportunity for story and character development. The established producers and the exhibitors were the stumbling blocks.

I was prepared to offer Griffith a very large salary, perhaps fifty thousand dollars a year, a fantastic sum for the time and industry. The prestige of his film name, coupled with great stage names and plays, would cause the industry to sit up and take notice. And the longer picture would give scope to his genius.

Griffith was extremely courteous, but he said that he was not ready to leave Biograph. He was in high demand, and it may be that he regarded me as just another promoter painting the clouds. At any rate he was not interested even to the point of talking salary.

After Daniel Frohman joined me, I asked him to try Griffith once more, this time making the fifty-thousand-dollar offer. But still his response was negative. He told Frohman that even though he left Biograph he could arrange to make more than fifty thousand dollars. And in time he did. Later Griffith worked for me. But I have always regretted that we were unable to be together at the height of his powers.

Edwin S. Porter was more open to argument. Despite his old barnstorming life, he was a careful man, a Scotsman, I think, who saved his money and disliked risks. By that I mean he was distressed by the ups and downs and worries of business. His Rex Company was having only fair success, and I think he was intrigued with an offer to make pictures and let someone else worry about marketing them and meeting the payroll, while still having a chance at profits.

Yet he had many reservations. "You won't be able to get the plays," he said.

"Yes," I answered. "We will get them."

"If you get the plays, you won't get the players," he continued.

"We'll get them too."

People have said that I was a persuasive salesman, in a quiet way. Whatever the truth of that, I was persistent. Perhaps I was convincing because of my own faith. And now, risking the savings of my lifetime, I *had* to believe.

Porter remained full of doubt, but he was willing to join in as long as he did not have to put in any money. He would furnish his experience, talent, and prestige. Porter told me I should approach Griffith, whom he called the better director, and was not miffed upon learning that this had already been done.

Meanwhile I was making arrangements to launch *Queen Elizabeth*. Daniel Frohman offered the Lyceum Theatre for its premiere, or, more exactly, a showing for the trade and the press. This was of great importance, for to the best of my knowledge no major legitimate theater had ever been given over to a film showing. I designed posters with large photographs of Sarah Bernhardt, following the pattern of stage posters rather than gaudy movie bills. Then I hired a press agent and took space in newspapers and theatrical publications.

Frohman took it upon himself to bring distinguished persons to the showing, a task the more difficult because of the summer season—the date set was July 12, 1912—when most of them were at their summer homes or at the seashore. Frohman's reputation and enthusiasm were responsible for the many notables present.

Nearly every member of the audience had attended many stage performances of Sarah Bernhardt. Consequently there was a letdown feeling at the beginning, for her voice was sorely missed even though one knew it would not be there. It was evident that she was not at home before the camera and her gestures were more exaggerated than they need have been. The play dealt with the Queen's love for the Earl of Essex and scenes had been improvised to make up for the lack of dialogue. The difference between stage and screen was pointed up by the fact that at the end she took a curtain call.

The New York *Herald's* critic no doubt summed up the feeling of stage people when next day he commented on the film. "While it can add nothing to Mme. Bernhardt's fame that she has acted before the motion picture camera, future generations will be grateful to her that she has done so."

But I had seen—along with Daniel Frohman and others—a number of things which had not concerned the critic. To begin with, the audience had not been restless despite the hour and a half running time. The critic had looked too many generations ahead. He had forgotten that the vast majority of his contemporaries had never had, and would never have, a chance to see Sarah Bernhardt in the flesh. He was right about future generations being thankful for her appearance, though not for the reason indicated. Her performance was of historical importance because it went a long way toward breaking down the prejudice of theatrical people toward the screen.

Some years later when Sarah Bernhardt was playing in New York, I sent my card to her dressing room. Word was returned for me to come to her at once. As I entered she was bidding others to leave us.

She inquired, soon after the greetings were over, "Did you make any money on it?"

"Yes," I answered. "It was very successful."

She sighed. "I am relieved. It was my fear that you would lose heavily."

Then I explained the great value of her performance to the motion picture industry. She was surprised and happy.

The profitable marketing of *Queen Elizabeth* was, however, difficult. Exhibitors were angered by the demand for high rental prices—as much as fifty dollars a day.

"That is outrageous," Marcus Loew shouted. "No picture can be worth fifty dollars a day."

Even so, he bought the New York State rights, or

part of them. The Schenck brothers were beginning to see a future in longer pictures, but Marcus was bound and determined to die hard.

Gradually the exhibitors realized that the public would pay an increased admission price for *Queen Elizabeth.* Their eyes bugged out when the carriage trade appeared at the box offices.

In this connection I remember a complaint by one exhibitor. I had taken a small office in the Times Building —the rectangular structure in Times Square around which the news lights run nowadays—and this fellow came in and charged me with making trouble for him. It seems that a carriage load of fashionable people had driven up to his theater to see *Queen Elizabeth.* Surprised by this patronage, he had ushered them inside with considerable pomp. The film had barely started when an apoplectic old gentleman came roaring up to him. It turned out that the party had expected to see Sarah Bernhardt in person. The old gentleman seemed to feel that by shouting long and loud enough he could force her to come out on the stage.

The exhibitor told me, "Your show bills are too persuasive."

He was joking about his own anger. *Queen Elizabeth* had opened his eyes to the possibility of a higher class of trade with feature pictures.

Now I was ready to put on full steam in an effort to get our own features into production. A lot of steam would be required, because the obstacles in the path were many. We had to get the plays and the players and a studio. For *Queen Elizabeth* we had not needed a license from the "trust" because it was made abroad. For domestic production we needed the licenses.

It was at this time that I went to see Thomas A. Edison. He followed my reasoning carefully. Many in the Patents Company, he agreed, were more interested in the machinery—cameras and projectors—than in the pictures. He was impressed that Sarah Bernhardt had acted before the camera, and also by the fact that Daniel Frohman was making progress in his negotiations with James K. Hackett, John Barrymore, and even Minnie Maddern Fiske and Lily Langtry.

Once Edison saw the possibilities of feature pictures, he became enthusiastic. Certainly, he said, they were worth a trial, and he would be glad to send a letter to Jeremiah J. Kennedy, head of the "trust," asking a hearing for me. Edison dictated the letter while I sat by.

After waiting long enough for the letter to be delivered, I called at the offices of the "trust" and applied to the receptionist to see Mr. Kennedy. One historian has written that I cooled my heels for seven hours in the anteroom. But that report is exaggerated. The wait was hardly longer than three hours. The discourtesy was not intentional, for I was not considered of enough importance to justify discourtesy.

Patience has always seemed to me more than a copybook virtue, and I decided that here was a good time to be virtuous. When at last I was remembered and given a hearing, Kennedy was polite but cold. He sat behind his big desk, looking every inch the captain of industry, listening with some impatience while I recited my arguments.

"No," he said, "the time is not ripe for feature pictures, if it ever will be."

7

IN the eyes of the "trust" I was an outlaw. While the independents were managing to survive, it was a painful fact that to succeed I would need to show in the theaters licensed by the "trust." For a "trust" house to screen an independent, or outlaw, picture meant seizure of its patented equipment and inability to get any more "trust" film.

Outlaw or not, I determined to go ahead, with faith that success of feature pictures would force the "trust" to license my products.

Edwin S. Porter's gloom remained thick, but Daniel Frohman was enthusiastic. He set his sights on James K. Hackett and *The Prisoner of Zenda,* in which Hackett was touring for him.

Hackett, still a reigning matinee idol though in his middle forties, was a big handsome fellow, well suited to heroic roles. His father, James Henry Hackett, had been a celebrated actor before him, known especially for his portrayal of Falstaff. The younger Hackett, formerly married to the lovely British star Mary Mannering, and now to the equally beautiful Beatrice Beckley, also English, carried on in the old theatrical tradition. He was rather on the flamboyant side, a high liver, a renowned tippler.

In the beginning Hackett contemptuously thrust aside the suggestion of playing in the flickers. When confronted with Sarah Bernhardt in *Queen Elizabeth* he began to weaken. Frohman, an old friend, asked pointedly how if the Divine Sarah was willing to appear before the camera, he could hold himself above it. We also argued that he owed it to his public which could see him only rarely on the stage. His need for cash was another factor in his acceptance.

We had trouble, too, in securing the film rights to *The Prisoner of Zenda*. The author, Anthony Hope, an Englishman, feared that the film would interfere with stock-company portrayals. Eventually motion pictures did kill off stock, but we argued that the picture audiences would want to see the actors in the flesh. Doubtless the lump sum of money offered, along with a belief that few would see the picture anyhow, was more effective.

For our studio we needed more space than was required for making short films. It was also a good idea to have it in or near midtown Manhattan to accommodate stage players.

After looking high and low, we rented the top two floors of the old Ninth Regiment Armory at 213-227 West Twenty-sixth Street, between Seventh and Eighth Avenues. The old drill space, without pillars, gave us a studio 100 by 200 feet. There were already skylights in the curved roof and we added more. The sun was the main source of light for picturemaking, as it had always been. We installed a few banks of lights to help out.

Workmen fell to. They threw up thin partitions for tiny offices at one end of the top, or shooting set, floor. Atop the offices, making a double-decker, they built a small projection room and a cutting room, connected on the outside by a narrow runway reached by a ladder. The shops of the carpenter and scene painter were at the other end.

The floor below was occupied by the laboratory, cubbyhole dressing rooms, and the prop and costume departments. Frohman let us have the costumes of *The Prisoner of Zenda* stock company, which was fortunate, since our costume department was bare. I made a deal with the owner of a Brooklyn theatrical shop to outfit us as best he could when the need arose.

Al Kaufman moved from the Comedy Theater to the studio as manager. Al was not to be judged on his barring of Mary Pickford and his slugging of Dutch Mack, though such abilities might come in handy on his new job. As outlaws, we were fair game for the snoopers and raiders of the "trust." Porter had, I believe, a Pathé camera. Even if in the clear on it, some of the other equipment might be debatable in court action. And by the time we had finished battling half a dozen injunctions, our heads might be too far under water for us ever to emerge. The studio was therefore closely guarded.

Al's greatest abilities were as a diplomat. One of the

first things he did was to ascertain Hackett's favorite brand of whisky. Then he filled a bottom drawer of his desk with bottles of it.

"Now," he told Hackett, "if any problems arise, please come in and talk them over with me. If I can't straighten them out, we'll go on in to Zukor."

Al was to get us over many hurdles with the aid of a few rounds of Hackett's favorite brand of whisky.

For our publicity man I chose a smart young fellow named Ben P. Schulberg. That name is well known in the industry, since he became one of the major producers. At the time we were getting under way, late in 1912, he was in his early twenties, a newspaperman who recently had been doing publicity for Porter's Rex Company. Schulberg's job was more than getting space in the newspapers. The whole purpose of the feature play was to raise the level of motion pictures, and it followed that we needed a dignified approach to the trade and public. Our policy was to make only the promises which we could fulfill. Schulberg's booklets and other literature gained a respectful hearing for us. Our pictures were issued, incidentally, over the trade name Famous Players Film Company. But we widely publicized the slogan: "Famous Players in Famous Plays."

In charge of the laboratory was another young fellow, Frank Meyer. He had never been in a film laboratory at the time he took on the job, but, since technicians were available, I was willing to sacrifice experience for a strong belief in feature pictures. Frank had been manager of a film exchange, and every time I had rented a film which told a story, we had remarked on its drawing power. Recalling these conversations, I asked him to join us.

Meyer went ahead energetically, enclosing the laboratory with galvanized iron and working out other methods of guarding the precious film negatives against fire.

Soon after I had announced *Queen Elizabeth,* a young film salesman named Alexander Lichtman called on me. Though little more than twenty, he was, like me, a veteran of Fourteenth Street show business, having carried water trays in Tony Pastor's vaudeville theater. His enthusiasm for *Queen Elizabeth* ran so high that I had sent him on the road, where he had great success in selling it. Now I hired him as our sales manager.

In making *The Prisoner of Zenda* we got off to a slow start. That was natural, considering the fact that neither Hackett nor his wife, the feminine lead, had ever played before the camera. The rest of the cast had been picked up here and there, with an effort made to secure experienced stage players. Al Kaufman spent a good deal of his time hanging around outside the Lambs' Club, buttonholing actors. He had no easy time hiring players, their prejudices against the screen being what they were. Our salary offers of from fifty to two hundred dollars a week, according to the size of the role, worked a number of wonders.

Hackett's fee was five thousand dollars, or in the neighborhood of tweve hundred dollars a week, since we expected the picture to be finished in a month. The total budget was estimated at forty thousand to fifty thousand dollars. Though tiny compared with the multimillion budgets of today, it was three or four times the sum ever spent on a picture in America. Most one-reelers were ground out on a budget of a few hundred to a thousand dollars. The fact that each of our five reels would run nearly ten times the top figure shows how much above the average we were paying for cast, authorship, scenery, costumes, and the rest.

The morning we started shooting is vivid in my memory. Porter, cigar clenched in his teeth, strode moodily up and down, hands clasped behind his back. One of them held a script he had dictated. It consisted of a few pages of notes to himself, and would be of no value to the players. On the studio floor he had drawn chalk lines, mapping out lanes which ended in circles. These were to guide the players into camera range.

Every once in a while Porter glanced apprehensively at the door through which Hackett would emerge from the dressing floor below. Finally he walked over to where Dan Frohman and I were standing.

"You say this Hackett isn't temperamental?" Porter asked.

"Not very," Frohman answered. "He may be a bit nervous, and it would be wise to handle him with kid gloves. But he will co-operate."

Porter walked morosely away.

Frohman said to me, "How about your man?"

I shrugged. "More temperamental than he looks."

"Let them work off the rough edges between them," Frohman said.

Finally Hackett appeared wearing the costume of the King of Ruritania, but walking with the air of a man being led to the gallows.

Probably everybody is familiar with the story of *The Prisoner of Zenda,* either from the book or the film, since it has been remade a number of times. The hero plays the dual role of the king of a tiny country and of Rudolf Rassendyl, an Englishman related to him through some shenanigans of their ancestors. Circumstances require the Englishman to masquerade as the king, who is held captive in the castle of Zenda. While doing so the Englishman falls in love with the Princess Flavia. It is all very romantic and improbable, but, as the remakings prove, good entertainment.

Hackett walked over to us. His handsome face was gray and I noticed that his hands shook a little.

"You got me into this," he said accusingly to Frohman. "And probably you've made a complete fool of me at last."

Frohman answered soothingly, "Jim, this is a historical moment. You're starting on the first feature picture ever made in America."

Hackett shuddered. "It's too early in the morning for jokes. Let's begin."

Beatrice Beckley, his wife, playing Flavia, appeared and they sat down with Porter while he explained the action of the first scene in detail. Earlier he had gone over with them the changes required to make the stage play fit the screen.

Hackett was ill at ease and this, with Porter's nervousness, created an atmosphere of strain. But they rehearsed the scene three or four times and it seemed to go off all right.

Then Porter took up his place behind his camera, which was about the size and shape of a small table radio and was mounted on a tripod. He had a small megaphone to speak through while cranking. The cranking speed was very important. No man's tempo was exactly the same as another's, and consequently if one cameraman started, he finished—unless there was a catastrophe. Porter had an assistant who could hit about the same speed, but he did nearly all his own camera work.

Frohman and I took places well in the background. My memory ought to be of a grand thrill as the camera was at last ready to roll in the initial feature production in America. Actually, I was inwardly tense and apprehensive.

Porter signaled to the players. They followed the chalk marks into camera range and began the scene—it was of the initial meeting of Flavia and the masquerading Englishman—which they had played hundreds of times before. It sounded just fine—and they had completely forgotten that the screen audience would not be able to hear their voices. In a moment they caught themselves, but now their gestures were overexaggerated and completely unreal.

Porter stopped cranking.

I headed for my office, walking briskly like a man satisfied with the way things were going. Frohman accompanied me.

They continued for a while and then knocked off for the day. We had agreed that the best thing was to take it slow and easy. I braced myself for a visit from Hackett. But he heeded Al's suggestion, and Al quickly broke out a bottle from the cache in his bottom drawer. Frohman and I dropped in, and between the contents of the bottle and a few thousand reassuring words the matinee idol's spirits were lifted.

Later Al came in to see me. "Porter's in his office walking up and down, up and down," he said. "He is the glummest I ever saw him, which sets a new record for the human race. Maybe you better have a talk with him."

"No," I said. "These are top men in their respective mediums and they will work it out."

Each morning I went on the set, talking with everyone, inquiring about problems, reassuring, trying to reduce the tension. Daniel Frohman continued to drop in to lend the weight of his reputation. But those first days were discouraging.

The ice began to break the moment Hackett saw himself on the screen. He, his wife, Porter, Al, Frohman, myself, gathered in the projection room to see the first takes which Porter had thought advisable to show.

Hackett watched excitedly. "You know," he said when the takes were finished, "I can see a lot of things I did wrong. When I get the hang of it, I'll do much better."

For one thing, he looked younger due to Porter's excellent camera work. He was flattered.

"All right," Porter said, "we will do them over."

Hackett looked at him in amazement. "Won't that cost a lot of money?"

"Regardless," Porter answered, "if you can do a better job we will do them over and if necessary over again."

Hackett looked inquiringly at me.

I nodded. "If you are willing, we are willing."

From that moment Hackett's interest picked up. He and his wife kept asking, "When do we see the pictures taken yesterday?" While he had not exactly resisted Porter's direction, the lack of understanding between them had shown itself on the screen. Now he began to help Porter map out the action. He followed the chalk marks instead of forgetting himself and striding all over the set.

Now that we were without our daily round of crises with Hackett, others had feathers easily ruffled. Many a night I had dinner with a player at the nearby Castle Cave Restaurant, explaining that the camera technique was different, that Porter had to insist on certain ways of acting to bring the story across on the screen. The players were not particularly temperamental. They simply did not know what to do and were upset.

Porter kept to himself, and if disappointed or hurt would light his cigar and pace up and down. I did not interfere in the production, but there were points I had to get across, such as the best way to handle the people who complained to me. The best way to do this, I discovered, was to send Al Kaufman up to a rathskeller in which Porter ate every night. Usually his secretary and assistant ate with him. Al was a cheerful companion, welcomed everywhere. Amidst his banter at the rathskeller he inserted the ideas I had sent along with him.

Even when things were going smoothly the thought of what we called the time bomb was disturbing. We had planted it ourselves, or rather Porter had. He had written a scene in which Hackett swam the castle moat. Hackett did not know about it. In the play there had been much talk of moat swimming, but no water.

One afternoon Hackett arrived at the studio to find the moat waiting for him. As moats go it was not much, being a canvas trough filled with two or three feet of water. Hackett was to swim in his clothes. We had at least enough water to wet them and him.

Learning of the realism to be practiced upon him, Hackett sprinted into Al's office, intending to pause only briefly before proceeding to mine.

"What's the matter?" Al inquired, reaching for the bottle.

"I'm an actor, not a swimmer," Hackett roared. "I don't intend to paddle around like a dog in a pond."

"It's a shame," Al said. "I offered to double for you, but you know Porter. He's stubborn and he turned me down. Let's have one or two while we talk it over."

Al was a fellow ever willing to help. Later, wearing a pinafore and a blonde wig with curls, he doubled for Mary Pickford in an airplane scene.

The King of Ruritania sat down. "I am a humble man," he said, not very objectively. "And I have co-operated fully. But the line has to be drawn somewhere."

Al filled the glasses and they drank. Then they drank again. Hackett was, as I have said, celebrated for his capacity.

"Porter is an artist too," Al began after a while. "He has dedicated himself to his craft, just as you have to yours, and as you know he is a top man in it. He would never for one moment ask you to inconvenience yourself except that he knows the moat swim will improve the picture. You'll be a hit and he wants to make you a bigger one."

Elbows continued to bend. Al held on nobly, but his eyes were become glassy when I went in. Hackett was going strong, but he had mellowed. I applied such arguments as I was able to muster.

"All right," Hackett said finally. "I'll swim your damned moat."

Porter, summoned from his office, crushed out his cigar and got behind his camera. Hackett plunged into the canvas moat like a huge water spaniel and splashed its length.

"Now," he said, rising from the shallow water, "there will be no doing it over tomorrow or the next day. Let's get it right now."

He stalked majestically around the moat and plunged in again. All told he swam it four times.

We made an effort to give *The Prisoner of Zenda* a big send-off, as we had *Queen Elizabeth.* This time we rented a hotel ballroom for a press and trade showing. The favorable audience response was apparent at once.

The elaborate sets and costumes were telling and so were the night scenes made with "sepia" film, new at the time.

Soon after the film ended, I was called to the telephone. Either there was a coincidence or people were right about Jeremiah J. Kennedy's spies. His office was calling to say that the "trust" would license the picture.

The chief publication of the industry, *Motography*, commented: "Undoubtedly *The Prisoner of Zenda* will score a tremendous popularity wherever shown."

And it did.

Hackett, despite his age, might have become the first of the great movie matinee idols except for a curious circumstance. His father had married late in life and the marriage had been bitterly opposed by a wealthy sister. Relationships had been broken off. The elder Hackett died two years after the birth of his son, and his wife and the sister did not communicate. The younger Hackett was barely aware of his aunt's existence.

About the time of the making of *The Prisoner of Zenda*, Hackett's attorney learned that the aunt had died, leaving the matter of the inheritance uncertain. Naturally Hackett, who always needed money, told his lawyer to investigate.

It developed that Hackett was the sole heir. I recall going with him to the dead aunt's old brownstone house after the fact had been established. He rummaged about, and I particularly recall him finding a photograph of his father in an old trunk. He set it on a mantelpiece and was almost as surprised as I at the striking resemblance between father and son. He had not kept a photograph of his father and of course did not remember him.

A little while later Hackett invited me to dinner at his hotel. To my amazement, a large number of people—between fifty and a hundred—were milling about in a banquet hall waiting to sit down. I soon noticed that the guests did not appear to be acquainted with one another, and were as mystified as myself about the purpose of the occasion.

A moment or two after we had taken our dinner places, a great wave of happiness swept over the room. On each plate was a check. Everyone present, it turned out, was a creditor of Hackett's, some of them going back a long way. I had advanced him some money beyond his salary. The checks were drawn to the amount of indebtedness with 6 per cent interest added. It was as gala an occasion as one would ever care to see.

Hackett's new-found riches finished him with the movies, and, for that matter, ordinary stage roles. He had always wanted to be a Shakespearean actor. Now he was able to indulge himself, and he did, playing mostly abroad until his death in 1926.

Recently while thinking about Hackett I looked him up in an old *Who's Who.* He had worked diligently on the forms which the editors sent to him, with the result that his biography ran a whole column of fine print, one of the longest in the book. It reported, among other honors, that twice he was a guest at Buckingham Palace and that he was the first player ever received at New York's City Hall and given freedom of the city.

He failed to mention his role in the first feature screen play made in America, the event for which he is the most likely to be remembered. It may be that his recollection of the moat was too painful.

8

MUCH depended on striking while the iron was hot, and we began hitting some blows heard throughout the industry. The grand lady of the American stage, Minnie Maddern Fiske, went before the camera. So did the world's most celebrated beauty, Lily Langtry, and a second matinee idol, James O'Neill.

Mrs. Fiske was reputed to be hard to work with, and we expected temperamental eruptions when she and Porter faced one another. They got along fine. Much of the picture *Tess of the D'Urbervilles* was made at her country home. Although Mrs. Fiske was still a year or two under fifty, and Porter was himself in his middle forties, he spoke of her as "the Old Lady." This referred, I think, more to her dignity than to her age. They ended with respect for each other.

When James O'Neill played *The Count of Monte Cristo* for us, he was in the autumn of his years as a matinee idol. He must have been even older than James Hackett, for his son, Eugene O'Neill, after some years of knocking about at sea, was preparing to enter Professor George Baker's famous playwriting class at Harvard, on his way to becoming America's most celebrated playwright of a later era.

Naturally we all were anxious for our first close glimpse of Lily Langtry, the "Jersey Lily," whose beauty was celebrated in song and story. Born on the Isle of Jersey, she had first gained success on the London stage, but her fame had long since spread around the world.

Dan Frohman brought her to the studio for arrangement of the final terms. We gathered about with proper awe. Though now past sixty, much of her beauty remained—though her straight, but full, features might now have better been described as handsome.

I noticed Porter standing aside, studying her. I joined him.

He shook his head. "She won't photograph well. Too heavy."

I shrugged. "We can't turn the clock back forty years. Anyhow, the public wants to see the great Lily Langtry."

The vehicle which she had chosen was *His Neighbor's Wife*. Some critics would have it that the films introduced melodrama. They should look up the old plays.

Miss Langtry's role was that of a devoted wife whose husband, a colonel, is having an affair with his neighbor's wife. The neighbor, discovering the affair, tells Lily about it, and, to mix things up in a highly melodramatic fashion, demands that she elope with him or else he will shoot the colonel down. To save her husband Lily agrees but first accuses him and he begs forgiveness. The hour for the elopement comes and goes, and Lily, determined to save her husband's life at the cost of her own, puts on his military cap and cloak and steps from the house. The neighbor shoots, taking her for the colonel. The wound is superficial and everything ends happily.

Porter was right. Lily Langtry did not photograph well.

Each of these pictures was made in a space of about three weeks and the editing or cutting time was held to less than a week. We were frankly in a hurry.

The feature plays were causing eyes to open in the trade. One day I was visited by William Fox, the film exchange and theater owner. He wanted to join us, but I had to tell him that we were already set and didn't need any associates. Proceeding on his own, he eventually became a major film producer and his name is still associated with the industry as a component of Twentieth Century-Fox.

The attitude of the old line companies toward me was changing from pity to anger. Though maintaining I would eventually crash ignobly, they charged that features were stirring up the public to no good purpose. Colonel Selig rushed out a two-reel version of *The Count of Monte Cristo.* We took him to court and beat him, but nevertheless were forced to delay our version and some of the edge was taken off it.

Louella Parsons was a scenario writer for Essanay at the time and she reported in her book *The Gay Illiterate* that George K. Spoor devoted a good deal of his energy to scoffing at me. The attitude was general.

I was just turning forty and was full of vim and vigor. There was enough to do without worrying very much about hidebound producers. I had not forgotten, however, the things I had learned as an exhibitor.

It did not escape me that the blonde little girl with the curls, Mary Pickford, whose photograph had hung in our tiny Comedy Theater office, was appearing in David Belasco's *A Good Little Devil.* Here was a young actress capable enough to play for that renowned stage impresario. And as "Little Mary" she had captured the hearts of movie audiences. The combination intrigued me, to put it mildly.

Belasco was at the height of his career, but, though of a theatrical manner, was not hard to get to see. I had talked with him several times about buying some of his plays. Finally he came to the studio for a viewing of *Queen Elizabeth* and *The Prisoner of Zenda.* He congratulated me for raising the level of film production, but his stock companies were doing very well and he hesitated to grant permission for the use of his plays.

I was following *A Good Little Devil* closely and knew that it was doing only fairly well. Doubting that he would send it on the road, I offered one day to buy it and employ the cast.

Belasco shook his head. "No, I don't think so." But his voice was not emphatic, and he added, "I will think about it."

I waited anxiously.

He came to the studio from time to time to see the new films as we completed them. After one of the screenings he brought the matter up himself.

"Whether *A Good Little Devil* will make a successful picture is more than I know," he said. "That is your business. At any rate, I have decided to let you have it, along with the cast."

"Fine," I answered, concealing my elation to some extent. "We have faith in the picture and are willing to make fair terms all around."

He added casually, "I should add that Mary Pickford is tired and needs a rest. Mary was ashamed, you know, to come back to me after appearing on the screen. I was looking everywhere for her to play in *A Good Little Devil* when one day she telephoned my assistant to say hello, and apologized even for that. It may be that she prefers not to go back into pictures."

My heart sank.

"She is familiar with the role," I said casually. "It would be helpful if we had her."

"Her understudy will do very well."

"Maybe," I said. "Anyhow, perhaps I can have a conversation with Miss Pickford and we shall see."

Then the great impresario amazed me. "When you get the play before your camera," he said, "I will come down to your studio and help with the direction. I'd like the film to be as near the standard of the play as possible."

The offer was quickly accepted. Yet happy as I was

for Belasco's assistance, it was the getting of Mary Pickford which vitally concerned me.

Mary was not quite twenty, but she had been trouping since she was five. Her real name was Gladys Smith and she was a native of Toronto, Canada, the daughter of a workman who had died when she was four. There was another daughter, Lottie, and a son, Jack. Mrs. Smith took boarders to make ends meet, and one of them, an actor, offered to seek places for the two little girls in stock companies. He succeeded, and from that time on the Smith family was in show business.

Mrs. Smith eventually settled with her brood in New York City and they picked up work as they could. There were months of near-prosperity when all the children were employed in a touring stock company. And there were the lean days common to most players. At fifteen Mary got her first good break in Belasco's production of *The Warrens of Virginia,* which also included, in the role of her older brother, Cecil De Mille. Belasco frowned on Gladys Smith as a theatrical name, and Mary Pickford was substituted.

In the spring of 1909, when Mary was sixteen, the Pickford family (Smith was dropped by all) found itself "resting"—the theatrical term for unemployment. As funds ran lower and lower, the traditional contempt of stage folks for the motion pictures lessened. One afternoon Mary took carfare money from the tiny hoard and went to the Biograph studios on Fourteenth Street.

There was no casting that day, but it happened that D. W. Griffith was passing by as Mary applied. In his eyes the perfect heroine was a young, innocent girl with yellow hair. He hired her, and she appeared first as a bit player in a six-minute comedy titled *Her First Biscuits.* She was one of those who suffered from a bride's first baking.

Soon Mary rose to "stardom" and thirty-five dollars a week. Charlotte noticed that "Little Mary" was gaining favor with screen audiences. The Pickford family voted unanimously that Mary was worth fifty dollars a week. When Biograph entered its veto, Mary sat down and wrote a letter to George K. Spoor in Chicago, offering to work for Essanay for fifty dollars a week. Spoor countered with a forty-five-dollar figure and they never got any closer together. Carl Laemmle was wiser. Before long all the Pickford players—including an in-law—were working for IMP.

The in-law was Owen Moore, with whom Mary had eloped. Moore was a rising young actor who had also been with Biograph. Charlotte Pickford was apprised of the marriage only after an IMP company was aboard a vessel sailing for Cuba to make a picture. It was a stormy passage, but Mary was always able to handle her share of a storm.

After my talk with Belasco I got in touch with Charlotte Pickford. She consulted Mary and they agreed to have lunch with me at Delmonico's.

I was waiting near the entrance when they arrived, and of course I recognized Mary from the screen and stage, even though her light hair was now done up in braids about her head. Her large blue eyes, studying me, were grave as we exchanged introductions. She might have been taken for any wholesome, pretty girl. Though her manner and dress were those of a young lady on a business mission, one felt the warmth of her personality and realized that in her gamin roles she portrayed another side of herself.

Mrs. Pickford was a buxom, comely woman with an open, good-humored face. "Mary liked your picture in the trade papers," she said as the waiter took us to our table. "She said you have long eyes like an Indian chief's."

I laughed. "That's why she is studying me so closely. I won't ask whether she is disappointed."

After we were seated, Mary spoke frankly. "I have about decided not to go back to pictures," she said. "Perhaps I'm building dream castles, but I feel that Belasco will star me."

I answered earnestly, "Motion pictures can aid your stage career. The atmosphere is changing rapidly."

And, as the food was served, I got into my "famous players in famous plays" argument. It was now vastly strengthened by my ability to point to the reigning celebrities who were appearing before the camera.

"Even Belasco," I said, "as you can see, is in the process of changing his mind about motion pictures."

I went further, speaking of the enormous untapped audiences which had never even seen stock. The success of feature pictures was demonstrating, I said, that great careers would be carved in this new field. The industry was very young. The crude techniques were giving way to improvements.

"The screen public will choose its favorites," I continued. "There will be a star system rivaling—maybe outshining—that of the stage. As for money, we have shown with *Queen Elizabeth* and *The Prisoner of Zenda* that people will pay higher prices for better entertainment. Big salaries are not a dream, for we have already begun to pay them—have been roundly denounced in the trade for it. If feature pictures succeed—and of this I have no doubt—we expect to pay according to drawing power at the box office."

Charlotte Pickford was impressed, I could see. She was a very realistic, far-seeing woman. It happened that Mary's stage voice was adequate, but not great. If my thesis held, then Mary, having already proved herself on the screen, had a bright and lucrative future there; a better one than on the stage. After the Pickford family's years of struggle, it was natural that the mother desperately sought security.

"What salary," Mrs. Pickford inquired, "would you consider paying to Mary?"

"Several hundred dollars a week," I answered. "Our program calls for producing as rapidly as possible. If theaters are to replace the one-reelers with feature pictures, we must provide them in sufficient quantities. I will pay Mary several times what she ever earned in pictures, and a great deal more than at her stage peak."

"We'll talk it over," Mary said.

I had made the best argument I knew how, and there was nothing to do but wait.

A few days later Mrs. Pickford telephoned. They were ready to talk terms. In the subsequent negotiations Mary's price was five hundred dollars a week for the time the picture would be in production—a fantastic sum for any but a famous stage player—but I did not quibble. I knew her value for the future, and I expected to be paying her more than that before we were finished.

The story of *A Good Little Devil* concerns a noble boy who, upon his mother's death, is sent to his uncle, a lord, to be reared. The uncle, having recently lost an only son, hates all children and places the boy with a heartless aunt. Here he meets a charming little blind girl, who is, of course, Mary. Both children love fairies and see them everywhere. The boy grows up to take his place in the world of lords and ladies, and becoming a snob, forgets the blind little girl. Then come some dramatic changes of heart. The aunt, sorry for her cruelty, begs her former charge to visit her. He does, and, finding that he loves the blind girl, renounces the world of snobs.

As a vehicle for Mary it was satisfactory. Unfortunately, Belasco's assistance of J. Searle Dawley in the direction—Dawley had joined us as Porter's assistant—was not beneficial. He insisted that the stage play be followed closely, with the result that much of the time the characters merely stood before the camera and talked. Belasco did, however, agree to an introductory scene in which he was photographed directing Mary. We made excellent use of this in our publicity and it was helpful in our overall struggle. But the picture did not do very well.

The really important thing was that Mary Pickford was now convinced of a successful future for feature pictures and Famous Players. She signed a contract for a flat five hundred dollars a week for a year. In that time we would make eight or even ten pictures, and from the receipts know where we stood.

I packed up prints of the five features we had completed—this was in the summer of 1913—and took them to London. Exhibitors showed enough interest to convince me that a profitable foreign market could be developed. The change of dialogue titles to other languages was, of course, very simple.

After returning in the fall, I announced that during 1914 Famous Players would make thirty feature pictures. This was twenty less than I felt necessary, but Porter said that production of fifty was out of the question. Thirty was fantastic enough, in his opinion, calling for two and sometimes three pictures in production at a time. There wasn't much studio space, he pointed out, and the lack of sun in winter added to the difficulties.

"All right," I replied, "we'll send a company to California for the winter sunshine."

The stir which feature pictures were making in the industry is shown by an editorial in the trade paper *Motography*. "Now it is known," the editors said, "that it was the amazing popularity of Famous Players' early subjects that attracted a number of other film producers to the feature field."

The magazine said also: "When the inevitable historian writes the history of the film industry, he will record Adolph Zukor as the apostle of the feature, the immortalizer of the visual half of the celebrated players of the day and the creator of a new and important branch of a new and wonderful art."

The apostle was not so confident as he may have sounded. I shoveled all the money I could find onto the small blaze. I hired more directors and cameramen, and searched frantically for scripts. I knocked on the dressing-room doors of stage stars, and, waving money as if I had a lot of it, begged them to come before the cameras.

The production pace had to be maintained, and Porter, Mary and Charlotte Pickford, and I went to Hollywood to open a studio. Why Hollywood? There was no particular reason. It was an undeveloped suburb of Los Angeles, mostly orange and lemon groves. The chief attraction was a rentable farmhouse suitable for dressing rooms, a small laboratory, and offices. We threw up a rude stage at what is now the corner of Sunset and Hollywood Boulevards.

Mary has charged from time to time over the years that in the beginning she was classified as a *B* player—and that, had she known it, she would not have signed her contract. It is true, at any rate, that since she was not a Famous Player she had no backlog of plays suitable to her talents. In fact, we arrived in Hollywood without a story.

Porter's office was the farmhouse kitchen. We sat

around it trying to think of a story. Mary told one which Porter rejected.

"Well," Mary said, "I have a better idea, but I read it in a magazine and I don't know which one, nor the title, nor the author's name. If we use it, all we can do is wait for the author to protest and then pay him."

She related the tragic tale of a little Spanish girl cast adrift on a forlorn island. After a while a man swims in, exhausted. His yacht overturned and he is sure that all the others, including his wife, were lost. The two fall in love, say a wedding ceremony over themselves, and live happily. A child is born. It turns out that the wife did not go down with the yacht, after all, and she appears after years of searching. The Spanish girl, forgotten in the happy reunion, clutches her baby to her bosom and hurls herself into the sea.

"We'll call it *Hearts Adrift,*" Mary said.

The story did not exactly fit a blue-eyed girl with blonde curls. But it was made anyhow, while I hurried back to New York and tackled other problems. The author showed up, all right, and got his money. The picture flopped.

We followed in Hollywood with Mary in *Tess of the Storm Country,* a tremendous hit that played back to some houses as many as seven or eight times. It established Mary, and, I often think, did as much as anything else to lift Famous Players onto the high road.

9

I AM not one to while away many hours longing for the "good old days." But those at the Twenty-sixth Street studio were wonderful and can never be repeated. The old-timers always speak of us as having been a happy family. We were fond of one another, but there is more to it than that. In the creation of something new there are always high spirits.

Recently I ran into Richard Murphy, then the head of our little "art"—really scenery painting—department, who is still working at his trade, although on a larger scale. Murphy brought out a photograph taken at a stag beefsteak dinner held in the early spring of 1914. My eyes grew misty as we went over it, identifying our old co-workers.

There was Dan Frohman, of course, looking dignified in spite of the little apron such as we all wore. Porter's mustache was wider and more pointed, I think, than was customary. I have already mentioned some of the others —Frank Meyer, Al Lichtman, Ben Schulberg, Al Kaufman, J. Searle Dawley. Other key men in the photograph are James Kirkwood, actor and director; Hugh Ford, a noted director from the stage; Bing Thompson, a director formerly with Vitagraph; Francis Powers, another director; Bill Marshall, Bill Marintelli, and Emmett Williams, all cameramen; Jack Stricker, carpenter; Bill Riley, property man; Al Kramer, electrician; and Dick Murphy.

Nearly all were young, yet most were film veterans. Murphy had been present the day D. W. Griffith arrived at the Edison bent on selling a script. Porter had taken one look at the strapping youth and told him to put the script back in his pocket—he was the leading man in *The Eagle's Nest,* to go into production within the day. Murphy and Riley had rigged up a hinged eagle which they manipulated with wires as it fought off Griffith as he climbed a peak to save a baby which the bird had stolen. Griffith's career had almost ended right there, for the wires got tangled and nearly hanged him. Later he had gone to Biograph.

Murphy was thankful, when he came to the Twenty-sixth Street studio, for the progress being made in techniques. At Edison and later the Rex, where he and Riley had gone with Porter, the camera had been chained to the floor to prevent vibration. It was easier to move the set than the camera when an angle change was wanted. Porter, always meticulous, occasionally had Murphy move a set a distance as little as six inches.

There was plenty to keep Murphy busy without joggling sets. He might be called upon to turn a table into a piano with the aid of some cardboard and paint. If a rug was wanted on the floor, Murphy or his men painted it. On canvas backdrops he created gorgeous castles, lowly dives, forests, streets—whatever was needed.

Murphy painted realistically, but there was a limit, and this led to a good deal of trouble with John Barrymore, a perfectionist and a temperamental one at that. Barrymore did not really want to be an actor. His idea of the good life was to paint in his Greenwich Village studio. That is, some days. In the nighttime and the remainder of the days he liked to romance and to roister.

Then in his early thirties, he was doubtless the handsomest man in the world. Every theatrical producer wanted him and consequently he was unheedful of the pressures many stage producers were bringing on players to keep them out of pictures. It was my custom to call on him in his dressing room, or wherever else I could find him.

"Jack, I have a screen play for you," I would begin.

He always listened in moody silence while I outlined it, and he rarely answered yes or no. After a while I would send one of his friends to him for his decision.

Once on the set, Barrymore was all business. He insisted on his way of doing things and sometimes there were flare-ups of temperament, but he gave his best and demanded that everybody else do the same. He preferred a story which combined romance, swashbuckling, and comedy.

Our major battle with Barrymore was over his determination to jump through a stained-glass window. His first pictures were *An American Citizen* and *The Man From Mexico,* but the window trouble came a little later. Murphy and Riley had secured a beautiful stained-glass window from a church which was being torn down. We always kept our eyes out for wrecking crews. From an old mansion, for instance, we might get a balustrade or an attractive doorway which added realism to a set.

The Barrymore script called for him to jump through the stained-glass window to escape a cuckolded husband who was approaching. After the real window had served its purpose for the camera, Murphy substituted a painted one for the leap. The moment Barrymore saw it the war was on. He was not going to jump through any painted window. It wouldn't look real. If he had to act to make a living, then he was going to do it right.

My desk was almost demolished by his pounding on it. I argued, as had everyone else, that he would hurt himself. He didn't care. To drive home his point he quit work. It may be, of course, that he felt the need of a bender. Whenever an actor or director became particularly temperamental over some lack of props and stalked out, we often suspected that he had something else in mind.

Finally Murphy and Jack Stricker, the carpenter, built a new window, substituting a resin composition for glass. The windows were set up side by side. From a distance they looked about alike—to everyone except Barrymore after he had come in for an inspection. He started to leave.

"We can put them both in the set within camera range," Murphy said. "When time comes to jump, you can take your choice."

I stood by listening to what to me was an excellent solution. It was my custom to go on the sets every morning, greet everybody, and circulate, hearing the differences between actors and directors and trying to resolve them. On this morning, after hearing Murphy's appeal to the impassive but haggard Barrymore, I went confidently into my office.

A tremendous crash brought me running out. Barrymore was picking himself up from the debris of the glass window. He looked happier than before, and he hadn't a scratch.

Quite a little noise was required to bring me out of my office, since weird things of all kinds were going on all the time. An incident in another Barrymore play lifted me out of my seat, though that was nothing to its effect on Frank Meyer in his laboratory on the floor below. The villain of the script had planted explosives under a house, intending to kill the heroine. Barrymore was to rescue her and carry her down a flight of stairs just before the house was destroyed. We needed to show only the stairway blowing up.

Murphy and Riley planted dynamite under it, covering the explosive with dirt. They may have used too much dynamite and anyhow did not know that dynamite explodes in the direction offering the most resistance. The charge blew a hole in the floor, which was also the ceiling of the laboratory. A chunk of wood barely missed Frank Meyer.

John Barrymore was an innocent participant in that affair, of course, and I do not want to leave the impression that he made trouble for us on purpose. But his beginning of a picture was a signal for us to go on the alert. Barrymore was fond of Al Kaufman and Al would accompany him on the town at night in an effort to get him home early, or fairly early, and to bed.

Once in bed, Barrymore was never in any hurry to get up. And when he did get up, he was likely as not to forget all about the film and begin to paint. Al's job was to go down to Barrymore's Greenwich Village studio, plead with him to arise if he were still in bed, and try to get him in a mood to come in. He was not always successful.

After Barrymore had been missing both from our studio and his for a few days, I would say to Murphy and Riley, "Go over to the waterfront and see what you can do."

Their custom was to begin at a favorite saloon of Barrymore's on Twelfth Avenue. If necessary they traced him from dive to dive. The effect on the prop and scenic departments was not good, but they often brought their man back.

It is possible to look back with amusement at these things. But at the time they could bring us close to disaster, for money was short, and often we were working on a picture that had been sold to the distributors in order to get funds to make it. And owing to lack of studio space we had to plan production with extreme care, tearing down an old set and building another overnight so that a different cast might start a new picture.

At one of these crucial points Barrymore did more than disappear. He shanghaied the director, in effect.

At the start of the picture I had offered a deal.

"Now, Jack," I said, "you can choose your starting time up to noon—if you'll promise to work eight hours once you do begin."

"That's fair," he said.

I added, "We'll be hurt badly if this picture isn't finished on time. It would help a whole lot if you stayed on the wagon."

He extended his hand. "A deal."

We shook and I knew he meant it. The picture was almost completed when noon came and went one day and there was no Barrymore. Al went to his Greenwich Village studio. Murphy and Strickler made the waterfront rounds. He was not to be found.

Finally James Kirkwood, who was directing the picture, offered to try his hand. He was a close family friend and knew better than the others how much was involved.

"I think he's hiding at The Players and won't come to the phone," Jim said. "If he's not there, someone may have wind of him. I'll go over." Kirkwood was a member of the famous actors' club on Gramercy Park and a close friend of Barrymore's. "If I find him, I'll drag him back by the neck."

"Oh, no," I said, "don't take a chance on damaging that profile."

An hour later Kirkwood telephoned. "I've got him and he's coming back with me."

Three days went by and neither one of them appeared.

What happened, it turned out, was that Barrymore had agreed to return on condition that Kirkwood stop with him at the Biltmore Hotel while he had one drink. Kirkwood consented. Barrymore ordered two absinthes —the powerful drink now outlawed in this country. Kirkwood didn't want any, but Barrymore, one of the most persuasive men in the world when he wanted to be, prevailed. One thing Kirkwood didn't know was that when the Biltmore bartenders saw Barrymore coming they always fixed doubles. Those drinks were the start—but not the last.

If any testimony is ever required to keep absinthe outlawed, I intend to step forward and supply it with fervor.

The studio favorite was Mary Pickford. Rather than an actress rising to stardom, she was to the Famous Players family a favorite sister and daughter. Mary had her hand in everything, writing scripts, arguing with directors, making suggestions to other players. But everyone knew she did it for the benefit of the picture, and her ideas were helpful. There is no doubt about her tremendous drive for success and the cash-register nature of a segment of her brain. I am convinced that Mary could have risen to the top in United States Steel, if she had decided to be a Carnegie instead of a movie star. But there was no caste distinction in the studio, and

Mary was the least likely to try to establish one. She was sincerely interested in the people about her.

There was the time Emmett Williams, her favorite cameraman, had a toothache and everyone was trying to get him to go to a dentist. Williams had come over from the Biograph studios, where he had learned "Rembrandt lighting" from Billy Bitzer, Griffith's cameraman. Earlier the light had been thrown on a scene from the front. Bitzer had placed lights behind the subject, getting a softer—or Rembrandt—effect.

Mary worked for many days on Williams before getting him to a dentist. It was too late. Infection had set in, and he died. Mary was badly broken up and did not come to work for a while.

Mary's warmth of sentiment was something used by Kirkwood—who directed many of her early pictures—to advantage. There were no satisfactory artificial tricks for making a player weep. For some scenes Kirkwood helped Mary to cry by picking a quarrel with her. But these were usually little-girl scenes where she was supposed to be angry anyhow.

For the more tragic ones he cleared everybody out of earshot, put doleful music on a phonograph, and sat down to talk to her. He recalled sad incidents in her life until finally she wept. Then the cameraman was signaled.

Sometimes Mary and Kirkwood played jokes on her mother. Charlotte Pickford was always there, sitting in on story conferences, watching her daughter's career like a hawk. Mary and Kirkwood would begin a scene in which Mary appeared to a disadvantage. Spotting it in a moment, Mrs. Pickford would call a halt and a big argument would ensue. Finally Mary and Kirkwood would give up with a great show of reluctance.

In time Mrs. Pickford gained a reputation as a great salary negotiator, and I can testify that it was well earned. But I wish all the "screen mothers" were like her. She was aware that fame is fleeting, that a player must work hard to keep it, and, failing, should have resources to fall back on. The Pickfords lived on a close budget whatever their income. Charlotte was an important and loved member of the studio family, jolly, helpful, sharing her wisdom in an unpretentious way.

The stage was set for trouble, one might have thought, when I brought in exquisite Marguerite Clark to play roles similar to Mary's. This was particularly true inasmuch as Marguerite's manager and older sister, Cora, was every bit as determined and capable as Mrs. Pickford. Marguerite was only four feet ten, a pixie with huge lovely eyes and a luxuriant mass of brown hair.

Curiously, Marguerite did not care to be a star. She did not dislike acting. She was merely indifferent to fame.

The Clark sisters, daughters of a Cincinnati businessman, had been left alone when Marguerite was a small child. Cora was about fifteen years the elder. Because Marguerite was in great demand for children's plays, Cora decided on a theatrical career for her. The two went first to Baltimore, where friends got a role for Marguerite. With seeming effortlessness she rose to lead billing.

I recall being first struck with Marguerite in a photograph of her in the stage play *Prunella.* Then one night I went to see her in *Merely Mary Ann* and decided to take steps to hire her for Famous Players. Daniel Frohman saw the Clark girls, but got nowhere. And so I appointed Al Kaufman to stick to the case.

Al spent a good deal of his time haunting back stages when not hanging around outside the Lambs' Club buttonholing players, chaperoning Barrymore, or, almost incidentally, managing the studio.

The results were sometimes curious. One night Al got into the dressing room of a big star—it seems to me it was Mrs. Leslie Carter—and offered ten thousand dollars for three- or four-weeks' work in a picture. Daniel Frohman's name was on Al's card for the purpose of opening doors to him. Next day the star telephoned a warning to Frohman that a crazy man using his name was making fantastic money offers.

Al went backstage at *Merely Mary Ann* for seventeen consecutive nights. Cora always barred him from seeing Marguerite. But Cora liked his persistence, and finally a conference was arranged between the girls and me. I offered one thousand dollars a week. That was fine as far as money was concerned. The hitch was that I wanted Marguerite to sign a three-year contract. I wanted to build her, like Mary, as strictly a picture star.

Years later Cora explained how our differences were finally adjusted. "I told Marguerite," she said, "that pictures were a fad and in three years would be dead. Therefore she might as well sign."

Marguerite never returned to the stage.

The building of motion picture stars was a very delicate thing. In many cities, curiously enough, the wise thing at first was to build Marguerite *down.* We were not aiming at her stage followers, as we had at those of Sarah Bernhardt, Mrs. Fiske, and Lily Langtry. We wanted exclusive moviegoers to get acquainted with her in roles we thought most suitable. Marguerite nearly always played the vixen who got into trouble through impudence and excessive high spirits, but won out in the end. She was popular, too, in fairy tales.

Marguerite was not lazy, but it was Cora who provided the vast energy and backbreaking work which went into the creation of a star in those days. Cora helped select the plays and coached Marguerite in every detail. I had made a rule that the stars read and answer their fan mail after we had made an analysis of it. Cora searched the letters to discover what the audiences liked best about Marguerite and saw that she answered them.

There was some rivalry between Charlotte and Mary Pickford on the one side and Cora on the other. Marguerite was not interested. But the rivalry was friendly and like that which exists in families. When Mary put on a new costume she might go ducking and weaving and hiding about the set, pretending to be avoiding Cora's inspection. Now that I think of it, we did try to have only one of the rival parties making a picture at a time.

I had voluntarily increased Mary's salary from five hundred to one thousand dollars a week. This was not owing to rivalry with Marguerite, though the Pickfords would have had a good deal to say had it not been done. The box-office receipts showed that Mary's pictures justified the increase. When players asked for more money, I invariably replied, "Let's look at the books." Since the pictures went to the public as soon as completed, we could make quick judgments.

Screen audiences, we knew from our fan mail, box-office receipts, and audience watching, favored little-girl players. Children identified themselves with them—directly in the case of girls and as playmates in the case of boys. Adults saw them as younger sisters or daughters.

Our very smallest girl was Marie Doro, who had been successful in the theater, especially in *The Morals of Marcus.* We produced it on the screen and starred her in others.

In connection with Marie I recall particularly a Buddha that Dick Murphy made for one of her pictures, *The White Pearl.* It was an example of the ingenuity required in those primitive days. The carpenters built a rough framework and Murphy fleshed it out with newspapers soaked in glue. Then he painted it and inserted a great "pearl" in the forehead. It was quite a majestic Buddha.

Pauline Frederick was a different type, tall and dark. Her neck and shoulders were regarded by artists as the most beautiful in the world. She was a few years older than the others and a player of more sophisticated roles. But there was nothing aloof about her at the studio. Her former husband was an architect and from him she had learned to draw. She used to sit with Murphy in his tiny office, helping design sets.

Others who had, or were to achieve, stage or film reputations came and went. Among the actresses were Elsie Janis, Hazel Dawn, Lois Weber, Ina Claire, Florence Reed, Bertha Kalich, Laura Hope Crews, Lenore Ulric, Charlotte Walker, and Fannie Ward.

Besides Barrymore, the male leads included Henry Dixey, Arnold Daly, H. B. Warner, Tyrone Power (father of the current favorite), Victor Moore (the renowned comedian), and William Farnum.

Farnum was outstanding in "he-man" roles which he played to the hilt. When he started slugging, other actors were never sure where his fists were going. One of the best scenes with Farnum resulted from some special casting by Al Kaufman.

The scene was laid in a barroom and Farnum was to throw bottles—it was before the day of breakaway bottles—and flail his fists in a berserk way. The extras, fearing Farnum would lose control of himself, had no desire to participate. Even if they had done so, they would have behaved in a wooden fashion. Al said he would fix it. He knew that Farnum aimed his blows.

Al went down to the street where a crew of a dozen or so Italian laborers were digging up the gas mains. On inquiry of the foreman, he learned that wages were $1.50 a day.

"All right," Al said. "During lunch hour bring them up to our studio. They will be in a motion picture, but all they have to do is sit around and drink beer. I'll pay you three dollars and each of them a dollar." He showed his money.

At noon they came up, stacked their picks and shovels, and took places at the tables of a barroom set. An actor in waiter's dress served beer, and, to make them feel at ease repeated a time or two.

Farnum dashed in and began hurling bottles every which way. In the excitement the laborers failed to notice the cranking camera. Some ducked under tables, others tried to restrain Farnum. He swung wildly. A few actors rushed in and took falls. Farnum didn't hit anybody, but the natural reactions of the amazed laborers were well worth the money. They had another round or two of beer and departed happily, a bit stage struck.

It had run through my mind that Farnum was engaged in the biggest uproar of all, but, on looking it up, I find it was Arnold Daly. He was playing in *The Port of Missing Men.* The script called for a scene behind Cooper Union, down near the Bowery, with Daly haranguing a crowd of derelicts.

Al went down and repeated the trick he had worked with the Italian laborers.

"Get a couple dozen of your friends," he told a likely looking character. "Have them behind Cooper Union at two o'clock and there'll be a dollar apiece for everybody. It will take about an hour."

Daly and Hugh Ford, the director, and a cameraman arrived to find a throng of two hundred or more Bowery veterans. Ford, knowing only that Al had arranged for some extras, was excited by the possibilities which the big crowd made for the scene. A property man distributed clubs of various sizes and shapes through the body of men. Ford had the cameraman shoot from many angles.

As they were finishing, a clerk from the business office arrived to pay off the extras. He had forty dollars, prepared for a slight excess of Al's calculation.

Our people held an emergency council. Daly addressed the throng again, trying to explain that a message was being sent to the studio for more money. It was no good. The Bowery men had seen the camera loaded into the automobile. They wanted no promises.

It was too bad that the camera had been put away, for the surging, roaring crowd had the making of a wonderful scene. The car was surrounded and the occupants were in real danger. Finally the police arrived and cleared a path.

After the party arrived back at the studio, we debated what to do. Though desiring to pay all the extras, we had no way of identifying them. If we went down to the Bowery we might find ourselves distributing cash to every derelict who was there or could get there. It would be like watering a desert.

Suddenly we heard a commotion down in the street. I ran to the window. Somehow the crowd had discovered our address—perhaps Al had left his card—and had hiked the mile or so from the Bowery. The men still had their clubs. It was reminiscent of a movie-shot of the storming of the Bastille.

We always kept a bundle of small bills for paying

extras. Fortunately, there were enough. We took everybody who was handy down to the street, established a kind of cashier's office, formed a line with the help of the police, and paid everybody.

I told Al, "You recruit up at the Lambs' Club as well as you do on the Bowery, and we'll have all the talent we need."

10

As the staff of Famous Players increased, Porter, though still directing, spent much of his time improving camera techniques. Porter was, I have always felt, more of an artistic mechanic than a dramatic artist. He liked to deal with machines better than with people. In a way it was his mechanical imagination which had caused him to improvise the story technique in *The Great Train Robbery.*

Porter was working hard on improving the fade-out. I recall a three by five foot glass tank which he used for endless experiments. He filled it with water and photographed through it while a man stood by and sifted colored powder into the water, which was stirred by a fan. Gradually the scene faded out—or, more exactly, was enveloped as if by clouds rolling in.

It may come as a surprise, with all the current excitement about three-dimensional films, that Porter was experimenting with them nearly forty years ago. He used two cameras, just as two or more are used now, and threw the pictures on the screen by means of two projectors. He had made a lorgnette with red glass for one eye and green for the other. Seen with the naked eye, the pictures were a hopeless swirl. The lorgnette gave them three dimensions.

I followed Porter's experiments closely and encouraged him. But we were ahead of our time. There was enough to do to put across flat, silent pictures.

Most of the old-line companies were still bitterly opposed to feature pictures. At first glance, their refusal might appear to have been to my liking. It was not. If a theater manager decided on a policy of feature pictures, he required a sufficient number to change bills at given intervals. We could not produce enough. Therefore I would have welcomed features from the older companies.

We were gaining access, it is true, to a backlog of stage plays. One day Dan Frohman came to me with the information that his brother Charles needed money and might listen to an offer for his old plays. Dan thought $25,000 a good round sum which would interest Charles. I scraped together the money. At what Dan considered the right psychological moment he laid a check for that sum on his brother's desk and made the offer. It was accepted. About the same time we made arrangements with the Henry W. Savage Company, another large producer, for its plays. No matter the supply of material, we could not produce fast enough to satisfy the market.

Luckily a few small new companies were entering the feature picture field. It was in the winter of 1913 that

Jesse Lasky, Sam Goldfish, and Cecil De Mille made their initial film under the banner of the Jesse L. Lasky Feature Play Company.

The organization of the firm on the back of a menu was, as I said earlier, the concrete beginning. It appears, however, that Lasky and Goldfish (hereafter I will call him Goldwyn, since that is the name he won fame with) had discussed the subject fairly extensively between themselves and Arthur Friend, who became company treasurer.

The ambitious and energetic partners decided to make *The Squaw Man* as their first venture. As lead player they secured Dustin Farnum, a stage figure. But not even Goldwyn, the sensational glove salesman, was able to talk Farnum into settling for a share of the profits. He wanted five thousand dollars in cash, and got it. As it turned out, he would have been far better off with a percentage.

De Mille, an athletic, balding young man of thirty-two, set off with Farnum and a few others for Flagstaff, Arizona. They arrived in a snowstorm and kept on going to Hollywood. There they rented a low barn, converted the horse stalls into dressing rooms, built a stage outside, and hired some Indians and cowboys. Shooting began on December 29, 1913, and thus the company was in Hollywood while we were at work on Mary Pickford's *Hearts Adrift* and *Tess of the Storm Country*. I did not, however, meet De Mille at this time.

Sam Goldwyn had remained in New York, handling the company's financial affairs while continuing his glove business. Goldwyn's youth had been a hard one, perhaps harder than mine. Born in Warsaw, Poland, he had run away to London following the death of his parents when he was eleven years old. In London he worked in a blacksmith shop until, a couple of years later, he made his way to America.

Goldwyn, about De Mille's age, was also balding. He was tall, slender, extremely meticulous in his dress, and so dynamic that glove buyers were hard put to resist him.

Jesse Lasky had stayed in New York too, keeping the vaudeville business going for himself and De Mille to fall back on in case the picture was a failure. Lasky, a showman to the core, was in his early thirties also. At twenty he had prospected for gold in the Yukon—and had been lucky to raise passage back to his native California. Later, stranded in Hawaii, he had earned his fare home by playing in the Royal Hawaiian Band, the only non-Hawaiian in it. After teaming in vaudeville with his sister Blanche, later Goldwyn's wife, Lasky had managed Herman the Magician and became a vaudeville producer. The failure of his Folies Bergère cabaret had not been a small one—he dropped more than $100,000.

After seeing *The Squaw Man,* I wired my congratulations to Lasky. He telephoned and suggested lunch at Delmonico's—which was more than agreeable with me.

I found Lasky charming, with a musical, effervescent voice, and full of enthusiasm. We talked mainly of feature pictures, and I do not recall that any great pearls of wisdom were dropped. But the meeting was portentous for both of us, since eventually we were to become partners, and perhaps for the growth of the industry. It was reassuring to find so able a man as Lasky with the same kind of faith in feature pictures that I had.

I remember one little incident of the meeting. Lasky slapped his breast pocket as if looking for a cigar, and I handed him one. In those days I smoked eight or ten a day, blacker ones than now. The reason he was without a cigar, it turned out, was that he was trying to quit smoking. That little scene, Lasky without any cigars, slapping his breast pocket, and me handing him one, was to be repeated endlessly. Only recently at lunch, after forty years, the pocket-slap came, I unconsciously handed him a cigar, and he called my attention to the ancient ritual.

Another feature company had been launched by Hobart Bosworth, a well-known actor. He had purchased the rights to Jack London's *Sea Wolf* and had himself appeared in the role of Wolf Larson. He followed with other London stories. The Oliver Morosco Photoplay company was another in the field.

The reader probably has little interest in corporate history, but a few lines of it will be necessary from time to time to make the story clear. The Paramount Pictures Corporation was not founded by me, though I was partly responsible. The organizers were a group of film exchange men led by W. W. Hodkinson, who represented exchanges in the Far West. Its purpose was not to make pictures but to distribute them. The year of founding was 1914, and the name was taken by Hodkinson from an apartment house he had happened to notice. Paramount's trade-mark, a mountain, was sketched by Hodkinson on a blotter.

An agreement was made by Paramount with several producers for distribution of 104 feature pictures a year. Famous Players agreed to provide 52, the Lasky company 30, and Bosworth, Morosco, and others the balance. The producer was to receive an advance of $35,000 on each picture and 65 per cent of the total receipts.

I was not entirely satisfied with the arrangement. It followed that in the end we would be advised—doubtless told—what kind of pictures to make. The distributors seemed to be in the driver's seat.

Let me quote briefly from Terry Ramsaye's *A Million and One Nights*, an extensive history of motion pictures. He said of this period: "Adolph Zukor of Famous Players was the most significant single figure in the field of motion picture production. He was inwardly driven by Napoleonic ambitions." The author continued: "When Zukor thinks, he walks. There was a night in this period that he walked from midnight to sunrise. Twice that night on the streets of New York he saw Battery Park and once he crossed One Hundred and Twenty-fifth Street. When the Sioux started ghost-dancing it meant trouble along the Big Horn. When Zukor starts walking it is time for everybody on the reservation to look out."

Mr. Ramsaye's two-volume study is an admirable effort to bring together the complex story of the movies. He was right when he stated that I often walk while thinking and certainly I did not believe that distributors ought to control production. Naturally I cannot agree with the reference to Napoleonic ambitions and assuredly I was never as dangerous as he implies.

Yet disagreements over policy arose and in due course the Paramount stockholders chose me to head the company. This was, I believe, owing to a conviction that I was best equipped to guide feature pictures to success.

Enough pictures were now being made to encourage exhibitors to build new theaters. In my opinion the construction program was one of the most important aspects of the industry. It was no good to make pictures if people must inconvenience themselves to see them. The Nickelodeon had fallen into bad repute. Many parents not only refused to attend but forbade their children to do so. If theaters were attractive, had comfortable seats and good music, an excursion to a picture would be a treat. The mood would be set for better enjoyment of the picture.

Mitchell Mark, my old associate of the penny arcade, was building the Strand Theatre, occupying the entire Broadway block between Forty-seventh and Forty-eighth Streets. His original plan was to depend chiefly on vaudeville. I had many talks with him, arguing that with a huge house such as his—seating 3,500 persons—he would do better with feature pictures. He was skeptical. For one thing, he did not think enough would be available. I finally convinced him, and the Strand, with an orchestra and a huge pipe organ, became the first great photoplay house.

As manager, Mark brought in S. L. Rothafel, the "Roxy" who was to leave as his monument the enormous

Roxy Theatre of today. Marcus Loew now believed wholeheartedly in feature pictures and was converting some of his houses to them. In California, I encouraged Sid Grauman to move to Los Angeles from San Francisco and open a movie house. The policy was to encourage the construction of movie "palaces," with financial assistance whenever possible.

Meanwhile Famous Players encouraged other producers of feature pictures. The first loan-out of a player, a common thing today, was of Marguerite Clark to Lasky for *The Goose Girl.* It was one of those plays in which a sweet little girl spends a lot of time in such bucolic pursuits as feeding geese. Mary Pickford wanted the role and was unhappy when I did not outbid Lasky for the play and doubly unhappy when I loaned Marguerite for it. But the important thing was the production of good features.

I was encouraged when D. W. Griffith, after leaving Biograph, gave the feature picture a lift with *The Birth of a Nation,* one of the film milestones. It was based on *The Clansman,* a novel, originally the picture title also, and dealt with the reconstruction period in the South. Being a southerner, Griffith was bitter on the subject of carpetbag rule. He did not think his picture slurred Negroes, but there was widespread criticism and he was charged with encouraging the Ku Klux Klan. Whatever the merits of the controversy, *The Birth of a Nation,* made in 1914 and released a year later, was a great success and drew new audiences to the movies.

At about the same time Griffith was making his epic,

we had in the works a spectacle of our own, *The Eternal City,* with Pauline Frederick. It was religious in nature and Porter took a company to Rome for many of the scenes, including some in the Vatican. In it Porter reached a new high mark with his camera work.

The budget of *The Eternal City* was $100,000, by far the most costly we had attempted, and through an oversight we faced one of our recurrent crises. One long sequence showed the hero pleading with the Pope during a walk in the Vatican gardens. Unfortunately, he clutched the arm of the actor portraying the Pope.

Only after the company's return did we learn that no one is allowed to touch the Pope in such a manner. It was therefore possible that Catholics might take offense. The matter was further complicated by the fact that Hall Caine, author of the book on which the play was based, had been an adversary of the Catholic Church. We cut as much as we could, yet some of the unfortunate scenes had to stay unless we were to postpone everything and send the company back to Rome. And extensive distribution plans had already been made.

I called on Bishop (later Cardinal) Patrick Joseph Hayes and explained to him that our mistake was an innocent one and we were sorry for it. I was reminded of the time I had stood outside the little theater in Newark, waiting to explain that the showing of the *Passion Play* was with the best of intentions. A ban by the Catholic Church on *The Eternal City* might put us out of business.

Bishop Hayes was sympathetic. We released the picture and there was no trouble. Afterwards the Bishop and I became good friends and often discussed the moral and religious implications of films.

Now trouble with Mary Pickford began to develop. Her shoes pinched her feet. Her costumes did not fit right. The directors were making unreasonable demands. The stories offered her were no good. This was not Mary's true nature, I knew. It was Mary's way of opening salary negotiations.

Also there were press reports of huge salary offers to her by another company, and the reports were true. The serials, or "cliffhangers," were becoming popular, with Pearl White leading the field in *The Perils of Pauline*. Mary was offered four thousand dollars a week to play a serial lead. It was a tight spot. I could not pay her anywhere near that much—and yet to lose her might be disastrous.

Nowadays Mary sometimes tells me that I spun out doleful stories during all salary negotiations. They were tales, she says, of a barefooted lad wearing a straw hat with a ragged brim peering hungrily into the window of a Ricse pastry shop, dreaming of the day when he would have enough to eat. My implication, as she saw it, was that I ought not to be made hungry again. I am not one to quarrel with Mary's recollections. Certainly we did a great deal of talking, usually over a dinner table as she and her mother bargained carefully.

Eventually Mary signed a new contract with Famous Players at $2,000 a week, half the figure offered by the serial company. It is hard to believe that my stories were worth $104,000 a year. There were more important factors.

Others, particularly Marguerite Clark, stayed with me when they might have got a bigger salary elsewhere. Marguerite later married a Louisiana businessman and became, as anyone knowing her charm would have expected, a favorite of New Orleans society. She is dead now. But Cora Clark is still vigorous and she was talking recently of our old negotiations. She was surprised, it seems, that I never had my attorneys present when the players came in with theirs.

She recalled one time that I said to her, "Please tell your sister to tell her lawyer to talk more slowly. My mind doesn't work that fast."

My request was serious, and I mention it because of its bearing on the salary deals of those days. Much depended on good will between player and producer, and upon mutual faith in our goal. This good will was not to be gained by the haggling of third parties. The players sometimes took less for the moment because they believed Famous Players' methods would bring them a greater income in the end. For example, Mary Pickford was not cut out for serials. She became convinced, as I was, that by halting our star-making program she would eventually be the loser.

After nearly three years of feature production, I was, in the autumn of 1915, reasonably confident of the future. In my office one evening I was toting up some figures and congratulating myself that we had piled up a backlog of half a dozen negatives for later release. There was no way to see the dark cloud of doom which hung over me.

Preparing to depart, I noticed a light in Frank Meyer's cutting room above the row of little offices. Frank was a strapping, good-humored fellow, but he had a worried expression on his face when I climbed the stairs and went in.

"Everybody's gone home," I said. "Why don't you be sensible and do the same thing?"

"Got work to do," he answered.

"In addition," I said, "you look sour. Did some director leave out a scene that you have to cover with your pencil?"

Frank wrote the captions as he cut, and he was always embittered when a director left out an important scene and he had to try to cover it with a bit of dialogue. He was particularly miffed at Hugh Ford, who liked to make horse-racing pictures. We lacked money for hiring horses and jockeys and consequently Ford would simply leave the race horses out.

"No," Frank answered. "I'm not sore at any director at the moment. Those building inspectors were around again. They claim my safe is too heavy and will drop through the floor. So I had it bolted to the wall. Now they say the wall and the whole building will come down."

He was very proud of a huge jeweler's safe that he had bought somewhere. Inside were drawers in which he stored the precious negatives.

"Go on home," I said. "After a good night's sleep you'll feel better and we'll worry about it tomorrow."

He shook his head. "I've got a few hours of work yet on Pauline Frederick's *Zaza* and I want to finish it tonight."

"Do whatever you please," I said. "As for me, I'm taking my son out to dinner and later to see the Packy McFarland-Mike Gibbons fight down at Coney Island."

Frank cut moodily away. "Go ahead. I've got enough fighting with those foolish building inspectors to keep me busy."

11

MY son Eugene and I had a pleasant, relaxed dinner at the Knickerbocker Grill. I was happy that Eugene, in his middle teens, was aiming at a career in pictures and worked at odd jobs around the studio when not in school. We hurried a little toward the end of the dinner in order to make sure of reaching the fight on time.

The September evening was cool as I slid under the wheel of my Pierce-Arrow touring car, lighted a cigar, and headed through Times Square down Seventh Avenue. The expensive Pierce-Arrow was self-indulgence, in a way, since I enjoy good things. I have always worn well-tailored clothes of excellent cloth and cut even when I have had to wear the same suit for five years. I have always believed that if a man surrounds himself with good things he sets a standard in his own eyes as well as those of others.

As we crossed Fortieth Street, Eugene leaned out of the car. "Look," he said. "A fire, and a big one."

Smoke and flame were rising at a point some distance

below us, and now a fire company flashed past, bells ringing. Whenever a man sees fire trucks heading into the area of his home or office he begins to worry, and I was no exception. A few blocks further along we ran into crowds. A policeman was ordering traffic to turn off Seventh Avenue.

"What's burning?" I asked the cop.

Obviously tired of answering questions, he waved me on.

"My office is down there," I insisted. Doubtless my expression caused him to relent.

"It's a movie studio."

The car lurched forward as I stepped on the gas.

"It's got to be ours," Eugene said after a little. "There's no other studio close enough."

I swung into Eighth Avenue and began looking for a space to park. "Yes, it's ours. Frank Meyer was working late."

We parked in the thirties and commenced to run. Now the flames were leaping high. According to the *Times'* account next day, the fire was one of the most spectacular ever to occur in the city. We headed into Twenty-sixth Street on a dead run and fought our way through the crowd to the police safety barriers. Ambulances were going through and others were coming out. Medical workers had thrown up a field hospital in the street. Firemen were being carried from the blazing building.

"Did you see her explode?" I overheard a policeman

ask another. "Must have been that film laboratory. All kinds of chemicals, likely."

I caught his attention. "Were any civilians brought out?"

"Don't know. You have somebody inside?"

There could be little question in his mind. I am not good at concealing deep emotions and was conscious of tears on my cheeks.

"Yes. May I go through and make inquiries?"

He nodded.

Telling Eugene to stay where he was, I ducked under the barrier and ran through the maze of hoses and other fire gear to the field hospital. Frank Meyer was not among the patients. I inquired about civilian casualties but learned from the feverishly working medics only that a few spectators had been overcome. No one had heard of a civilian escaping from the inferno.

Al Kaufman arrived with a friend of his, Winnie Sheehan, secretary to the police commissioner. They made further inquiries and checked the hospitals. There was no word of Frank.

By now the fireman had abandoned hope for the armory and were concentrating on neighboring buildings in an effort to hold the fire. We stood by and watched the studio crash down to a heap of blazing ruins.

And then I saw an amazing thing amidst the smoke. To the brick wall of the neighboring structure clung Frank Meyer's big safe.

"Well," Al said, "for that we're entitled to a drink. Now anything can happen." We went into the Castle

Cave Bar and in a few moments were bowled over again. Frank Meyer walked in, spic and span.

"My God," I shouted. "All the time I thought you were dead in the fire, and instead you had the sense to go home."

Frank smiled wanly. "I went home to clean up. That fire ruined my clothes, even though it didn't quite fix me."

It was established later that the fire had started in a braid factory on a floor below those rented by us. A barrel of benzine had been delivered to the factory just before the fire started. Apparently it had exploded, spreading the flames. The alarm rang in the studio only after it was filled with smoke.

Frank, hearing the bell, had dashed out to the little runway alongside the projection and cutting rooms. The smoke nearly gagged him. He heard the flames somewhere in the building. Turning, he found that the door to the cutting room had swung shut and locked.

He dashed along the runway to the projection room and re-entered the cutting room through a connecting door. Quickly he swept the negative of *Zaza* into the safe, which contained another negative of a Pauline Frederick picture, a couple of Mary Pickford's, one of John Barrymore's, and three or four others. He slammed the safe door shut and tried to lock it, but was not sure whether or not the bolts had slid into place.

The roar of the flames was louder now. Frank sprang up the stairs to the roof. It had recently been tarred and he slipped and fell as he made for the water tower at one corner. Up the ladder to the top of that he clambered as fast as he could and gained the roof of the adjoining building. As he did so, firemen on the street threw a stream of water through one of the studio windows. An explosion followed. Looking back, he saw the tarred roof burst into flames.

By the time Frank discovered a way down to the street, grime had mingled with the tar and the sweat of his exertion. He had gone to his home, which was not far away, to wash up and change clothes.

"Your safe is still hanging on that wall," I told him. "It was there a little while ago anyhow. Maybe the wall has buckled."

Frank rushed out and was gone for a few moments. "It's still there," he cried, returning. "Solid as ever. And the negatives are in good shape, too."

I looked at him, startled. "They'll melt."

"No, they won't. That safe was built to resist heat. That's the main reason I bought it."

I nodded. "Likely you're right."

Frank eyed me accusingly. "You don't believe me. But I say those negatives are in first-class shape and will stay that way."

"Why should there be any doubt?" I said. "We'll know in a few days when the embers have cooled and we can climb up there."

After a while I went outside and stood at the barrier, looking up at the safe. A large crowd continued to mill about. In it were Jesse Lasky and Cecil De Mille, who, hearing that a picture studio was afire, had come down for a first-hand view. At that moment they were standing only a little distance from me. De Mille and I were not yet acquainted.

De Mille's director's eye had caught something odd in the scene.

"See that fellow?" he said to Lasky, pointing to me. "Everybody else is in motion, if ever so slightly. That fellow stands absolutely motionless. He has something to do with this fire."

"He has, indeed," Lasky answered, following the pointed finger. "That's Zukor and no doubt he's lost everything he has in the world tonight."

They came over and Lasky introduced De Mille to me. We shook hands and, according to De Mille's later report, I fell back at once into my motionless observation of the safe.

"It's a terrible loss," De Mille said. "Perhaps there is something we can do to help."

"Thank you," I answered. "We start rebuilding tomorrow."

With nothing more to be done at the scene of the fire, I hunted up Eugene and we drove home. My wife was completely upset, I believe, for the first time since our marriage. I assured her that I had gone far enough with the feature pictures to know that somehow I would still win out. The loss would amount to several hundred thousand dollars—there was no doubt in my mind that the negatives had been destroyed—and only a minor part was covered by insurance. And greatest of all was the loss of time in the battle to put feature pictures across.

I sat down at the telephone and began making calls

to Mary Pickford, John Barrymore, Marguerite Clark, and other players, and to company officials and department heads. I asked each to be at the Astor Hotel on the following day to lay plans for carrying on.

Next morning I drove past the blackened, smoldering remnants of the studio. The safe still clung to the wall. I halted the car to study it. Wisps of smoke—doubtless from the film—appeared to be escaping from it. I drove grimly on.

The atmosphere at the Astor meeting was as heartening as anyone could desire. I made a little talk, stating my hope that we could go on. They rose one after another—Mary, Barrymore, Marguerite, all the others—to pledge co-operation.

After the meeting, Frank Meyer came up. "We can raise a scaffold to the safe in a couple of days," he said.

"Good," I answered.

Nothing was to be gained by telling him of the smoke I had seen emerging from the safe.

We took office space in a building on Fifth Avenue across from the public library, and, after searching the city, rented an abandoned riding academy on Fifty-sixth Street for a studio. In three years we had learned a great deal. But there seemed little doubt that now we started over from well behind scratch.

On the third day after the fire, just before noon, Frank Meyer's voice came on my telephone.

"She's open," he said.

The tone of his voice told me nothing. "Yes?"

He did not punish me further for my lack of faith.

"They didn't burn, they didn't melt, and only one is crinkled a little."

I said humbly, "My car will be down to pick them up."

That safe of Frank's was an important factor in saving Famous Players. To have remade the pictures would have been expensive and time consuming. With them we were able to satisfy in part the demands of the trade.

The wisps of smoke I had seen, it turned out, had come from a chimney behind the safe. During the fire a brick had come loose.

As it was, Famous Players' road back was steep, flanked by many dangerous precipices. Along the way, unfortunately, we lost Porter, who had been badly shaken by the fire. Hating business risks, as I pointed out earlier, he did not feel like going on. We agreed on a figure for his share—well in excess of half a million dollars—and I raised enough money to buy him out. Porter died in 1941, never having returned to movie production.

One of the movie historians declares that Porter lost his money in the stock-market crash of 1929 and later was found working in a machine shop. It is hard for me to imagine Porter taking chances in the stock market. As for him working in a machine shop, I suspect he was there tinkering with an invention of some kind. Porter was a fine man, a great pioneer, and his name richly deserves to be honored by the industry he helped to create.

12

FAMOUS PLAYERS continued to produce many pictures in New York City, to be near the stage players on whom we still depended heavily. But our Hollywood activities increased rapidly and I spent a good deal of my time there. This was not the boiling, roistering Hollywood of a few years later, on which we had to clamp a lid with might and main, and then sit on it. Pioneer Hollywood, rollicking with good fun, was our Twenty-sixth Street studio on a vaster scale. Excitement and adventure were in sufficient supply for all.

There was the adventure of Mary Pickford, Al Kaufman, and a "heavy"—the trade designation of the villain—named Douglas Gerard, in the affair of the airplane and the blonde wig. It was the first time a movie scene in a flying plane was photographed.

In the winter of 1915 Alan Dwan was directing Mary in *The Girl From Yesterday,* and Al had gone out to manage the Hollywood studio. The script called for a scene in which the heavy abducted Mary, bound hand and foot, in a speeding automobile. To Al this seemed like old stuff. He thought he had a better idea.

Rooming next to him at the Los Angeles Athletic Club was a young pioneer airman, Glenn L. Martin—later one of America's greatest plane builders. Al inquired of Martin if, should Dwan consent to shift the abduction scene from the automobile to a plane, he would fly his plane for the purpose. The cameraman would be placed on a cliff and the plane would pass him.

Martin agreed. Mary was excited by the idea of going up, and Dwan was pleased with the opportunity for a novel scene. Doug Gerard, older than the others, thought more about the risks involved. His mind began to dwell almost exclusively on plane accidents.

Had I been in Hollywood instead of New York at that particular moment, I would have sided, I am positive, with Gerard, in spite of Martin's great aircraftsmanship. But it was Al's and Mary's party, and Al talked Gerard into agreeing to fly.

A niche was found in a cliff for the cameraman, and the other preparations were completed. While he was about it, Al notified the newspapers, who sent photographers to make pictures of the take-off.

At the last moment Charlotte Pickford found out that Mary really intended to fly. She had thought the scene was to be made on the ground. She put her foot down hard. Now Al was on a spot, with the news photographers already on hand.

All of his and Mary's arguments to Mrs. Pickford were

unavailing, and finally Al sent to the studio for a wig of blonde curls and a young girl's dress. Then with Mary and her mother he went behind a house at the other end of the field and got into the wig and dress. Martin taxied down and picked him and Gerard up and then flew low past the news photographers, but not in good camera range lest the switch of personnel be noticed.

Al had never been up in a plane, and the swoops past the movie cameramen on the cliff scared him nearly to death, for he was sure a wing of the plane was about to hit the rock wall. In this case nearness to the camera did not matter, since Al, bound hand and foot, was struggling to get loose while Gerard held him down, and he could keep his face turned away. Close-ups of Mary's face would be made in the studio and edited into the scene.

Safe on the ground once more, Al found that his problems were not over. The news photographers were angry. They had no suitable pictures and were charging foul play.

Mary took over. "I'll go up if Glenn will take me," she announced simply.

Mrs. Pickford tried to put her foot down again. But now the affair lay between Mary and her public. She had agreed to furnish photographs of her flying in an airplane, and she would do it. Mary believed, rightly, that stardom is a two-way matter between player and public.

Finally Mrs. Pickford said, "Now Glenn, I'll let her go up if you'll promise not to fly above five hundred feet."

Martin laughed at the notion that a fall from five hundred feet would be less dangerous than from a thousand, but he agreed.

The newsmen got all the pictures of Mary taking off that they wanted, and of course this time Martin did not fly near the cliff.

Later Al discovered, to his dismay, that Doug Gerard had been more concerned about the flight than he had supposed. The night before, Gerard had written out a will by hand. In it he had left a diamond stickpin to Al.

A man whose spirit pervaded early Hollywood, with joy to all present and most of the rest of the world, was big, handsome Mack Sennett, known among his friends as the "Sensitive Boilermaker." He was known also as the "King of Comedy," a title richly merited.

I had the good fortune to be associated with Sennett and his merry men in the heyday of the Keystone Comedies, though he was well established before our association. Mack always did things in a large way and in a hurry. One characteristic was his faith in "the shake." The two of us would come to a general understanding on the production, financing, and distribution of his comedies.

"Now then," Mack would say, "the lawyers will put all this down on paper. With legal stuff a fellow can slip and squirm till doomsday. We've got our deal. Let's shake. Neither one of us will try to get away from that."

And we would solemnly shake hands. I felt good that Mack classified me as a man he could "shake" with.

A run-down of the names of those who played for Sennett is enough to set any old-timer to laughing. And many a youngster too, since many of his comedies are being revived on television.

Here is a partial list: Ben Turpin, Charlie Murray, Ford Sterling, Roscoe "Fatty" Arbuckle, Mabel Normand, Charlie Chaplin, Marie Dressler, Buster Keaton, Polly Moran, Slim Summerville, Edgar Kennedy, Wallace Beery, Charlie Chase, Mack Swain, Gloria Swanson, Harry Langdon, Hank Mann, Phyllis Haver, Rube Miller, Chester Conklin, Al St. John, Willie Collier, Harold Lloyd, Fred Mace, Marie Prevost, Louise Fazenda, Bebe Daniels, Hal Roach, Henry Lerhman—and Mack himself.

The Sensitive Boilermaker had indeed worked at the boilermaking trade under his real name of Michael Sinnett. The "sensitive" referred to his youthful determination to be an opera singer. Though his services were never demanded by the Metropolitan, his basso profundo was heard in a fashionable New York church, in a burlesque house, and on musical-comedy stages. Then, like so many others, he drifted into Biograph's brownstone studios on Fourteenth Street.

At Biograph he acted in comedies, took lessons in script writing from the always-helpful "Little Mary" Pickford, and studied the directing methods of D. W. Griffith. It was hard for Mack to write a script without putting cops into it. The comic policeman had been a stock figure since the peep show and the "modern" trend was to eliminate him or at least tone him down. Sennett held staunchly to a view that the single cop should be replaced by an entire police force.

Eventually Biograph allowed him to direct, but not until he headed his own Keystone Comedy studios in Hollywood was he able to put his police theories to the test.

Sennett presided over his sprawling jerry-built studios with outdoor stages and his restless band of comics from an office called the Tower. In it was an enormous bathtub and a rubbing board. He liked to hold story conferences while luxuriating in his tub or while his rubber, a gigantic Turk named Abdul, kneaded his ropelike muscles. One day a mild earthquake shook the Tower while Mack was on the rubbing board. The race of the towel-garbed King of Comedy, followed by Abdul, across the lot was an epic of the chase, though unhappily not filmed.

The making of a Keystone Comedy was a free-wheeling enterprise, with the script merely a jumping off point. Everybody from Sennett down took a hand. Directors and players were allowed to improvise almost at will so long as additional expense was not involved. If it was, they had to go to the Tower for a decision on whether the bit was funny enough to justify an extra cash outlay.

Mack's judgment of what would make people laugh was excellent, as the record demonstrates. But he is more apt to tell a story showing how wrong he could be, and one of them he told me recently illustrates the Sennett methods.

The script of a film in the works called for two escaped prisoners to be chased into a cow barn. The director appeared at Mack's bathtub with an idea. He wanted to throw a cowskin over the convicts, with the rear man holding down a rubber glove as the udder. The "cow" would get into a line of real animals and a nearsighted farm hand would come along and try to milk the glove.

The King of Comedy roiled the water morosely with his hand. "Too expensive," he decreed, "and not funny."

The director accepted with ill grace and went out and finished the picture. Thereafter he was never assigned to a story—a Keystone Comedy was rarely more than a day or two in the shooting—but that he called at the bathtub and fought Mack over including the cow scene. After a while he scored a hit with one of his pictures. Mack's usual bonus for a success was permission to include in a subsequent picture some creative bit hitherto denied. The director naturally chose the cow episode. Mack saw it in the projection room and was not moved to mirth.

Then a sneak preview audience laughed for three solid minutes, forcing the projectionist to stop the show. Later the director laughed for another three minutes at the King of Comedy, who filed away another reminder that no one can ever be sure what an audience will like.

Chief of the Keystone Cops, and Sennett's leading comedian in the beginning, was Ford Sterling, a trouper since twelve years old when he had joined a circus as "Keno, the Boy Clown." He was big and muscular, well equipped for knockdown, hit-'em-with-a-bed-slat comedy, which was Sennett's specialty. Sterling's big shoes harked back to his clown days. His job as head of the police department gave him plenty of opportunity for exaggerated facial contortions and slam-bang action.

The rank and file of the cops wore helmets, after the manner of the London bobbies. The helmets were more picturesque than the average American policeman's cap, it is true. But Sennett may have had something else in mind. His early backers had complained that the action in his comedies was too violent—therefore tone it down. Mack hated to do that.

One night he slipped into the counting offices and examined the books. Sennett comedies, he discovered, were doing exceedingly well in England. This knowledge strengthened his determination to hold out for violence. It may be that he employed the bobby hats as an expression of gratitude to the British, plus a feeling that the gesture would hold them in line in case another crisis developed.

The force's personnel varied from time to time. Those who stand out in my mind are big Edgar Kennedy, who later was to make slow-burn anger a specialty; slim-faced Charlie Chase, also to have a long career in comedy; tall, hound-dog-sad Slim Summerville; iron-jawed, menacing Hank Mann; sad-eyed little Al St. John, and Roscoe "Fatty" Arbuckle. It may be that Ben Turpin, Buster Keaton, and Chester Conklin served also, but I do not recall seeing them on the force.

Fatty Arbuckle was to achieve the greatest popularity of any of these. Though still in his middle twenties when he went to work for Sennett in 1913, Arbuckle had struggled for many years in the show business. At seventeen he had been a tenor singer of illustrated songs in a vaudeville house. After that, Leon Errol, who was managing a burlesque theater in Seattle, gave him a singing job.

Arbuckle then tried the screen with the Selig company, and, failing, toured for a number of years in shoestring musicals. It was after returning from a tour of the Orient that he found a job with Sennett.

Arbuckle weighed three hundred pounds and often ate three steaks and all the trimmings at a sitting. But most of his poundage was bone and muscle. A sedentary fat man could be funny, as John Bunny proved with Vitagraph. But it is doubtful that such a one could have worked for Mack Sennett. His men were athletes, and Arbuckle was the best athlete of them all. Once he entered a hundred-yard dash with some practicing college sprinters. They thought it a gag until he beat them. He was a powerful swimmer, able to leap out of the water like a porpoise.

Arbuckle could "take a fall" from a height of ten or fifteen feet, land on cement, and be up and running in a flash. Sennett and I were only recently discussing with awe Fatty Arbuckle's falls, but then the ability to take falls was a measure of a man's worth in the Keystone Comedies. It was not enough that a man could take them. He had to *like* to—otherwise he never would have survived.

Mack paid a fellow named Johnny Rand twenty-five dollars for each fall—in a day when an ordinary comic earned fifty dollars a week. Rand stood straight and fell rigidly over backwards, his head appearing to strike the ground before any other part of him. To this day a light comes into Sennett's eyes when he talks of Rand's falls.

Buster Keaton had become a part of his parents' acrobatic show when five years old, which gave him a good background. But it was his deadpan expression during falls that made him a finished artist. Around the Keystone studio it was believed, however, that cross-eyed little Ben Turpin got the most true pleasure out of a fall. He occasionally broke the boredom of a long streetcar ride home with a fall or two.

Sennett credits Ben Turpin and his feminine star, Mabel Normand, with introducing the thrown custard pie. A new director was trying to make Turpin laugh. Ben did not feel like laughing that day. On a bench Mabel noticed a lemon meringue pie which a couple of workmen expected to share for lunch. Practical jokes were the standard order of procedure at Keystone and everybody on a shooting story expected to be messed up in one way or another anyhow.

Mabel threw the pie with perfect control into Ben's face. He laughed good-naturedly and wiped the pie away. Onlookers thought Mabel had been nice to help the director, but otherwise paid no attention. As it happened, the cameraman had cranked all the while.

Sennett kept a rocking chair in his projection room, and the others gauged his reactions according to the movement of the chair. Vigorous rocking denoted pleasure. When the pie bit came on the screen he almost turned over backwards. The audiences bore out his judgment. Immediately the thrown pie was ranked with the fall and the chase as a Keystone laugh-maker.

Had Mabel Normand missed Turpin with the pie everybody would have been greatly surprised. For she was, though small and curvacious, a fine athlete. Mabel could swim, dive, run, jump, box, and—the really important thing—take a fall wonderfully. She was one of those rare comediennes—like Gloria Swanson, Clara Bow, Carole Landis, and Jean Arthur after her—lovely to look at and able to play dramatic roles. It has been maintained that Mabel Normand could have been the greatest dramatic actress of her period. But she was too full of the comic spirit for concentration on purely dramatic roles.

Mabel was an Atlanta, Georgia, girl who went to New York while in her teens to be a painter. The beauty of her soft round face, great liquid eyes, pile of dark hair, and petite figure was such that Charles Dana Gibson, James Montgomery Flagg, and other noted artists sought her as a model. At sixteen she became a player at Biograph, where she met Sennett. After the founding of Keystone she went to Hollywood as his leading lady.

It was Mabel's swimming and diving that gave Sennett the idea for his celebrated Bathing Beauties. Most of his comedy was based on some outcast who encountered one misfortune after another in trying to cope with life. By making one of these outcasts—say Ben Turpin—the darling of beautiful girls, Sennett got a contrast that was sure fire. Another basic ingredient was the fall from dignity—the Keystone Cops were, after all, a satire on pompous enforcers of the staid rules of society. Who could resist laughing at a handsome snob rejected by luscious beauties in favor of dead-pan Buster Keaton or enormous mustachioed Mack Swain?

Sennett did not hire all who came on his lot. But he hired a high percentage of them. From this constant panning of the stream he secured many gold nuggets. There was pretty Louise Fazenda, a schoolgirl who went on to be one of his stars. Later Gloria Swanson dropped in at the studio and was hired at sixty-five dollars a week. Others, like big Marie Dressler and little Polly Moran, came from the stage with reputations already made.

On the whole, Mack had better luck with those who had not already established a type of comedy. My old friend Sam Bernard, for example, was given so little to do during a contract stint that he brought in a bed and spent most of his time sleeping in it. Weber and Fields, Eddie Foy, and Raymond Hitchcock were others with big stage reputations who did not appear to the best advantage at Keystone.

Wage trouble with Ford Sterling was responsible for Sennett's screen discovery of Charlie Chaplin. Though Sterling drew $250 a week—a startling figure for comedians—he was threatening to quit and form a company of his own.

Sennett bought a new uniform for his police chief as a gesture of good will, and consulted his books. Then he called Sterling in.

"Ford," Mack said, "I've decided to go the limit and far beyond. My offer is $750 a week."

William S. Hart

Comdr. R. E. Byrd and Adolph Zukor

Barney Balaban

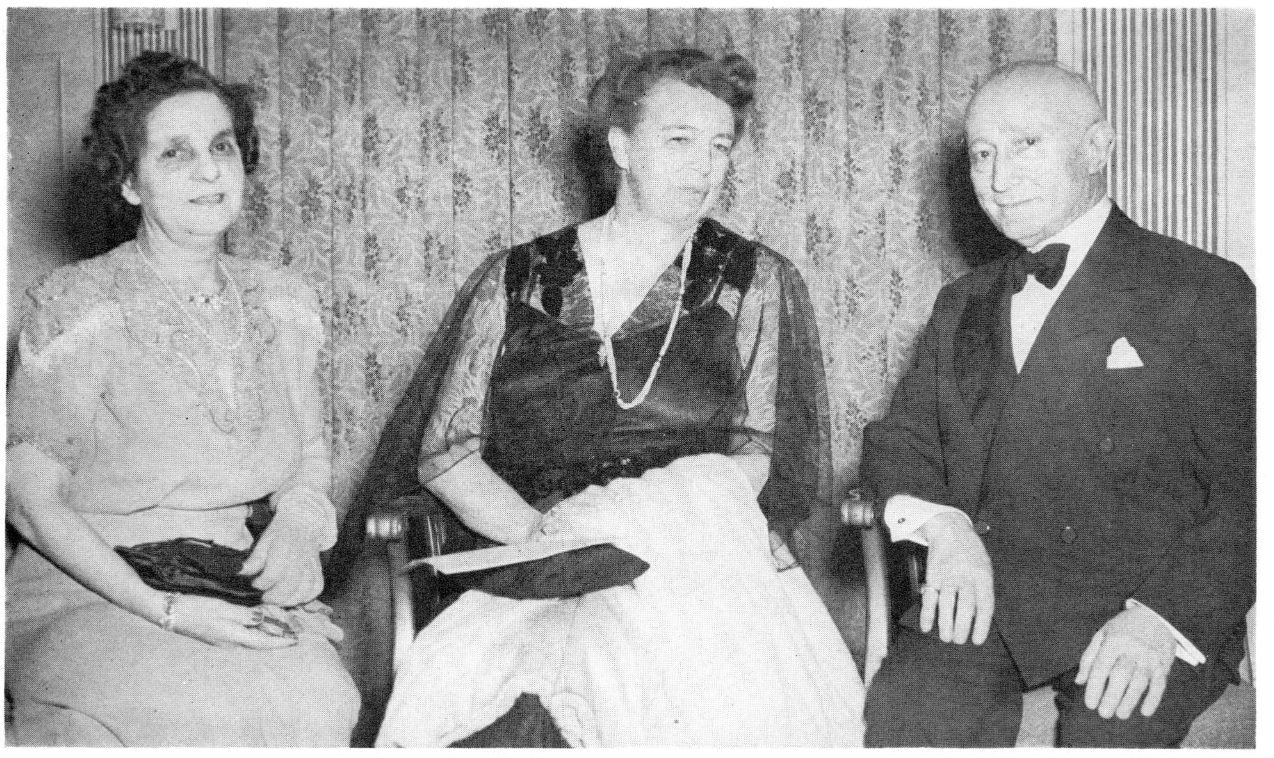

Mrs. Roosevelt with Mr. and Mrs. Zukor (1943).

Queen Mary and Adolph Zukor

Sterling tossed his new chief's hat into the air and danced a jig.

The King of Comedy relaxed comfortably in his bathtub. "No need to thank me, Ford," he said. "I'm glad you're staying."

Sterling halted in the middle of a jig step. "Who said anything about staying?"

"You act like a happy man."

"I am." Sterling clapped his hat on his head. "Anybody would be happy to know he's worth $750 a week. It ends any doubt that I can make a go on my own. I'm still quitting."

While Abdul rubbed and pounded the new kinks which promptly came into the Sennett muscles, the King of Comedy did some thinking. In New York, accompanied by Mabel Normand—there was a romantic as well as a business attachment between them—Sennett had attended a performance by the Karno Pantomime Company, an English troupe. The show was called *A Night in an English Music Hall.* Both he and Mabel had been impressed by a little pantomimist who acted drunk while watching the show from a box which had been built on the stage.

Sennett could not remember the fellow's name, though he thought it began with *C.* Perhaps it was Chambord or Chadwick. At the time he had discussed with Mabel the possible hiring of the pantomimist, but had done nothing about it. Now, desperate for enough talent to replace Sterling, he wired an eastern representative, giving the name of the company and describing the actor and his role, for help in finding him.

The representative caught up with the little Englishman in Oil City, Pennsylvania. Chaplin, it turned out, was booked solid at $50 a week. This was 1913, and he did not want to take any chances with the flickers. Sennett wired an offer of $125 a week. On the advice of the Karno manager, who told him he was never likely to earn that much on the stage, Chaplin accepted.

At first Sennett was disappointed. Chaplin, playing a kind of Desperate Desmond in a high hat and droopy mustache in his first two pictures, was a sorry flop. Everybody at Keystone experimented with new comic getups, and Sennett told Chaplin that he had better see what he could do. The comics were free and easy with each others' props.

Chaplin took a pair of Ford Sterling's old shoes and, the better to keep them on, put them on the wrong feet. Then he borrowed a pair of Fatty Arbuckle's pants. He added a coat belonging to Charles Avery, who was smaller than he. The derby hat was a stock prop, especially if too small for the wearer's head. Chaplin put one on. Mack Swain always had a supply of mustaches lying about. Chaplin tried one but it was too big and he kept cutting it down until it was only a dark blur under his nose. With the addition of a cane—the symbol of an outcast trying to gain status—Charlie Chaplin had the costume he was to make famous around the world. Audiences took notice of him at once.

With Famous Players showing the possibilities of the

feature-length picture, Sennett decided to try one. For it he hired Marie Dressler, who fitted the category of famous stage players, and she was the star of *Tillie's Punctured Romance.* Chaplin had only a featured part, but nowadays when the film is revived he is given top billing. Yet he rose fast enough, and in a year or two, after leaving Sennett for Essanay, he was the highest paid player in the business.

The robust comic spirit of Mack Sennett and his men burst out of his studios and rolled over Hollywood, and well beyond. In those days a favorite restaurant of film people was Al Levy's. There one might see the comedians deep in serious conversations, for the feeling of camaraderie was strong and none hesitated to help a rival with some knotty professional problem. Or, more likely, they would be engaging in high jinks. In that case—look out!

The best—or worst—trick played on me was, however, aboard a cross-country train. The comedians always made the diner their headquarters between meals, often pushing the tables aside for crap games. Fatty Arbuckle customarily engaged a boy to pick up the dice for him.

Arbuckle came to me late one afternoon. "Would you mind skipping your regular dinner tonight?" he asked. "Some of the boys are having a turkey cooked in your honor. We'll eat after the regular diners are through."

"Why, of course I'll wait," I said, trying to keep the apprehension out of my voice.

Buster Keaton was the waiter, when the time came. That boded no good. Yet he did a fine job until his proud appearance with a huge turkey, held high on a platter above his head. Arbuckle's foot somehow got in his way. The turkey rose to the ceiling, with Slim Summerville in a wonderful basketball center's leap after it. He tipped it to Ben Turpin, who batted it to Chester Conklin, and so on. Finally it rolled in the aisle. Arbuckle leapt headlong for it, somersaulted, and hurled it at me.

"Fortunately," I said, dodging the rubber bird, "my appetite is not strong tonight."

A real turkey was produced and Keaton, though taking some wonderfully narrow chances with the bird, did a magnificent job of serving.

By now the reader is doubtless asking, What happened to the old comedies? I must plead guilty to having been partly responsible for their demise, though inadvertently. Development of the feature picture was the handwriting on the wall. Sennett had started in the day of short films and his momentum kept him going as the features gradually took over the field.

It was not that theater bills lacked room for the comedies. The main trouble was that exhibitors refused to pay a high price for what became a side dish of movie fare. Therefore the comedians were not able to command high salaries and inevitably the best of the talent, old and new alike, aimed at the longer pictures. The double-feature and technical improvement in animated cartoons were the finishers, though a few short live comedies are made to this day.

13

ONE evening Mrs. Zukor and I were sitting in a New York theater waiting for the curtain to go up, when I overheard two men behind me talking in French. One of the voices, I noticed idly, had an American accent. The deep tone was suddenly familiar. My glance around drew the attention of the men.

I was looking into the long, tanned, steely eyed countenance of William S. Hart, the King of the Cowboys—wearing a dress suit.

We greeted each other. "I knew you could talk the Sioux language," I said, "but I had no idea you spoke French."

Bill Hart laughed. "Only fairly well," he answered. "I'm rusty and my friend is brushing me up."

I introduced Mrs. Zukor to Hart—though we were associated in business he had not yet been a guest in our home, as he often was later—and he introduced his friend to us.

As the curtain went up, Mrs. Zukor whispered to me,

"He's every bit as handsome in dress clothes as in his cowboy outfit."

And of course he was. That rugged face was striking under any circumstances. Certainly never another matched it for western pictures.

In his time Bill Hart had played Romeo and Hamlet. He was a cultured man—a deep reader, an author of books, a lover of the fine arts. From these facts one might jump to the conclusion he was slumming in western screen roles, interested only in the money. He made a lot of money. At one time his pictures grossed larger than any in the world.

Yet no actor ever more truly portrayed himself—or several sides of himself. On the screen Hart was honest and blunt-spoken. In real life he was the same—which doubtless inspired his novel about Patrick Henry. His physical and moral courage were as boundless off the screen as on. He usually played a lonely man—and Hart was lonely.

Nearly all of his pictures contained a scene in which, faced with some problem, he threw his arm around the neck of his horse and confided in him. Many went to a Hart picture for that scene alone. At his ranch Hart often walked with his horses up into the hills, pouring his heart out to them. He was convinced that they understood.

William S. Hart was the father of the western picture. Tom Mix was the better horseman, a more knowledgeable cowboy, and had entered pictures earlier. But Mix was not a big success until after Hart had established the western format. "Broncho Billy" Anderson, hero of the one-reelers, had been forced out of the competition.

Hart was an artist in his field, and he left his mark on the industry aside from it.

Born in Newburgh, New York, young Bill Hart in his boyhood roved with his family through Iowa, Minnesota, Wisconsin, and the Dakotas as his father, a miller, moved from job to job. When Bill grew a little older, he worked on farms and learned to ride. It was in the Dakotas that he became acquainted with the Sioux Indians and learned their tongue. He knew terrible adversity and suspense when for many years his father was on the verge of going blind.

When the family returned east, young Hart went to New York and worked at a variety of jobs while preparing himself for a stage career. At the same time he was an athlete, a member of the New York Athletic Club team. Curiously, taking into account his later screen life on horseback, he was a heel-and-toe man, a champion walker.

On the stage Hart had more than average success, especially in *The Trail of the Lonesome Pine, The Squaw Man,* and *The Virginian.* An experience of Hart's while playing a stage western role illustrates his pride and the lengths he would go to establish a point.

Miller's 101 Circus was playing in the same town. To whip up interest, the publicity men of the play and the circus began hurling taunts back and forth in the names of Hart and the 101 cowboys. Hart publicly charged—without being aware of it—that he could ride better than the cowboys. The cowboys said—without knowing anything about it—that he could not ride at all, was actually afraid of horses. The exchanges went so far that Hart, finally learning about them, believed his courage was at stake.

He went to the bunk tent of the cowboys and made a proposition. Next day he would come to the circus and allow them to watch him make up as an Indian. Then he would join his brothers, the Sioux Indians, in their saddleless wild riding act. He offered to wager that the audience would never know a white man was in the band. And he carried through, falling from his horse, remounting on the dead run, slipping over to the horse's side during a mock circling attack on a wagon train. The audience never doubted that he was a red man.

Hart went to Hollywood in 1914 to make two-reel westerns for Thomas H. Ince, one of the early independent producers. Then, as the feature film proved itself, Hart began to extend the length of his pictures. As I have said, he was a writer. This was important in his rise. So was the fact that he was over forty when he entered pictures. He had to create a character suitable to himself and was capable of doing it.

Generally speaking, Hart played the "good old man." He would start off as a desperado of some kind and then a set of circumstances or a good woman would put him on the right track. If not a desperado at the beginning, he had something else wrong with him. One of his titles, *Selfish Yates,* is an outline in two words of his type of picture.

Hart was the first to write explicit details into his scripts. In addition to being an extremely careful workman, he was dealing with rough cowboys from the range, unschooled in acting techniques. The westerns before Hart had consisted of little more than a few scenes—mainly hero with heroine, hero and villain shooting it out. Hart wrote an integrated story and saw that it was well told by the camera.

The horse-of-almost-human-intelligence, later a staple of all westerns, was first brought to the screen by Hart. This was hardly surprising, since he felt that horses were at least as intelligent as humans and probably more so. His favorite was a little white-faced pinto named Fritz. Bill's feet almost touched the ground as he rode. There was some criticism of so big a man on so little a horse, hardly more than a pony. But Fritz did not seem to mind and he could take sugar from Bill's pocket, untie knots, and look wonderfully sympathetic when Bill talked to him.

Fritz came between Hart and Thomas Ince. It was Bill's contention that Ince hated the pinto. He said he didn't know why and couldn't find out. Whatever Ince's side of the story, they had a fight over the use of Fritz in *The Narrow Trail*, one of Hart's early pictures. Ince lost. The pinto scored a hit and naturally Ince—who owned him—wanted Fritz used thereafter.

Hart's stubborn streak came out. He swore that Ince would never make a dime out of Fritz's talents, at least not from a Hart picture. He made his next fifteen pictures without Fritz. It was not until after Hart had come in with Famous Players that Fritz got back into action. Hart contended that Ince had underhandedly tried to hold him by refusing to part with Fritz. In the end, Bill claimed, he paid $42,000 for Fritz in the negotiations breaking off with Ince. He said the pinto was a bargain at twice the figure.

In the above I do not wish to imply that Hart was humorless. He ruled his cowboys with a strong hand, but there was always plenty of bunkhouse fun, and he participated in it. The cowboys often held kangaroo court and Hart liked to sit as judge or as executor of the punishment. He could take it too.

One time the cowboys hid a slipper belonging to blonde heroine Jane Novak, a star of others besides westerns, on a cabin rafter. Later Bill climbed up and got the slipper down. For this he was tossed in a blanket.

Another time he was convicted of loaning a heroine five dollars, which she lost shooting craps. The charge was that if heroines were to be loaned money, the sum should be a larger stake. The sentence was a "chapping" —a spanking with a pair of leather chaps. A young actor named Lon Chaney swung the chaps.

The most elaborate joke I ever heard of Hart playing had me as the intended victim, though others were involved before he was finished. Hart and I were warm friends. I enjoyed especially going on his set early in the morning—around six or seven o'clock—to talk with him while he made up. It was a relaxed time with few interruptions. The best jokes are played, of course, on friends.

One evening I had taken a train in Los Angeles for

San Francisco. An hour or so later, in the midst of nowhere, the train struggled to a halt.

Word flashed from car to car: "Holdup."

We looked out and in the light from the windows could see western bad men up and down the tracks. Passengers began to hide wallets and jewelry in the seats.

"They're only after the express car," someone said hopefully.

"No," another replied. "Too many of them just for that."

A tall man and a little man, six-shooters drawn, came into the car. The taller wore a slouch hat and a bandana over the lower part of his face. The shorter had on a huge sombrero and a mask. They headed for me.

"Hello, Bill," I said.

Those steely eyes were too well known to me. In his pictures Hart usually wore a hard-brimmed hat, more like a Canadian Mountie's than a sombrero. He had thought to disguise himself with the old slouch hat.

"Hello, Sid," I continued.

Sid Grauman could have wrapped himself in the Alexandria Hotel's Oriental rug and I would still have known him. Besides, in the event of a practical joke I always looked for Grauman at the bottom of it.

They announced at once to the other passengers that the holdup was a gag. But even after their departure many didn't believe it. The train crew had been in on the joke, of course, but I have always thought that Grauman and Hart and his cowboys took a long chance. Some passenger with a gun might have opened fire.

Action was the main theme of a Hart picture, and often he seemed to care more for his horse than for the heroine. An impression has arisen that he never kissed the girl.

"Bill always kissed the heroine at the end," Jane Novak told me recently. "He wouldn't miss that. Bill was writing the scripts."

In making *The Great Train Robbery,* Ed Porter had used a stunt man. In the era ushered in by Hart, the western heroes were their own stunt men except in rare instances. Hart told his men, "When I begin to slug, fellows, take care of yourselves." They did, and he took care of himself. Naturally they did not aim their hardest punches at one another's jaws, and probably nine-tenths of them went wild. But many a jaw was bruised.

In one saloon sequence Hart got into a knock-down-and-drag-out with a cowpoke fresh off the range. In an ad lib addition to the script Bill had ordered a scrimmage, with a break at a given point. In the ensuing free-for-all Bill landed a couple of stout blows on the stranger. Instead of breaking, the new hand charged with fists swinging.

Hart's long face clouded, lightning flashed from his narrowed eyes, and thunder rolled from his lips as he returned the attack. Finally other cowboys broke them up. The new man, it developed, was a deaf mute and had not heard the instructions.

Hart occasionally used a double, but Tom Mix never did. Prior to becoming a United States marshal and entering pictures, Mix had spent many years in Texas as a top cowpuncher and an authentic ripsnorter. He was a great joker—I recall him cantering his horse into the lobby of the Alexandria Hotel one time—but he had become a teetotaler. Whenever Mix made a scene in which he leapt from a second-story window to his horse's back, the cowboys would recall a time or two when he had done it in real life.

Mix did not allow any of his men to ride down a steep slope or jump his horse across a gorge until he had tried it first. For this reason, and because he was more knowing of range ways, he was more greatly admired by the cowboys than Hart ever was.

One day—to give an example of Mix's working methods—he was required to save Jane Novak from a herd of cattle which the villains had stampeded through a canyon. A perch for the cameraman was fixed on the almost perpendicular canyon wall.

"Now, don't worry," Mix told Jane. "When the cattle approach I'll ride my horse in, throw him, and pull you down with me beside him. The cattle will separate. No animal ever jumps over another unless trained to it."

He accomplished his aim with split-second timing and the cattle parted as he had said they would. Any slight failure on his part might have caused the death of both. Mix always maintained that he would live through his stunts and die falling from a rocking chair. He was killed in an automobile accident.

Even though Hart never matched Tom Mix in horsemanship, he faced many dangers. One night he and Fritz fought death together in a turbulent mountain stream. Hart and his cowboys, carrying torches, were to swim their horses across. Hart plunged in first. The swift water swept horse and rider into a whirlpool—a deep hole surrounded by an underwater slate ledge and a high wall.

They struggled wildly to get out. Three times Fritz tried to climb the wall, and three times fell backward. He swam into the submerged ledge and was buffeted away. The little pinto screamed in what Hart thought was almost human anguish, and as they battled for life Hart saw that Fritz' eyes were glazed. They sank together and it seemed to Hart that the end had come.

But Fritz fought back to the surface. Now Hart, his arm around the pinto's neck, asked for a last supreme effort. This time Fritz got his forelegs over the ledge. He struggled out, pulling Hart with him.

Hart was dedicated in his western roles, feeling that he was setting a good example for the boys of America. And he was right. Occasionally, though, he got so wrapped up that he was amusing. During press interviews he was apt to use cowboy language.

"Hi, little gal," he might greet a 200-pound woman reporter. Or to a male: "You old sonofagun, you're looking doggone fine."

After the interviewer had gone, Hart was likely to say to the publicity man with him, "Wal, pardner, that went off real smart."

"Look, Bill," the publicity man would answer, I'm from the studio. Remember me?"

Jane Novak accompanied Hart to the opening of a

picture in which they had played. After it was over, they retired to the lobby and Bill's fans were allowed to file past and grip his hand. Jane noticed grease spots on his vest and tie.

"Bill," she said later, "your vest is never spotted when you take me out to dinner. What's got into you?"

"Well," Bill answered. "It's this way. My public rather expects me to look common."

Curious, Jane made inquiries of Bill's devoted sister, Mary. Bill was a lifelong bachelor except for a marriage which lasted only a few months.

"I lay fresh clothing out for him whenever he goes to meet his fans," Mary said, distressed. "He dips his fingers into the gravy bowl and flicks gravy on his front."

Bill may have overdone the goodness of his screen roles, because there were a few adverse reactions. One time a rumor swept the fans of western pictures that Bill Hart beat his horses. No one ever told him. It would have been too cruel a thing to do.

Fritz seemed to Hart to become more human all the time. On location one time Fritz took up with a mare named Cactus Kate. Bill promptly bought the mare, and he told me afterward that she helped Fritz over many a rough spot. Hart had been informed that Cactus Kate was a bad outlaw, that no one had ever been able to ride her. He had her saddled and, mounting Fritz, led her on a jaunt of a mile or two. At what he considered to be the psychological moment, he had a cowboy mount her. Cactus Kate did not buck at all.

On location another time, a mule by the name of Lisbeth joined the party. Bill bought the mule too. The three animals were never apart after that.

Hart never claimed that Fritz could actually talk—at least in English to human beings. But Fritz was made to speak in a book which Hart wrote. It was signed jointly by the two of them.

One time when Hart checked in at the Ritz Hotel in New York, the clerk assigned him to the bridal suite, owing to lack of other space. Hart was amused and told me that he was in the "bridle" suite. When my daughter married, he sent a beautiful silver-mounted bridle to her as a wedding gift, knowing she liked to ride. It was her favorite for many years.

Bill played in the westerns until he was in his middle fifties, then retired to his fortresslike Spanish ranch house in the California hills. Fritz and Cactus Kate and Lisbeth died and he buried them with markers. To Fritz he raised a monument.

Hart was a great friend of James Montgomery Flagg, who illustrated his books. With the originals of these for a foundation, Hart began a collection of western paintings, including those of Charles Russell and Frederic Remington. He also collected the guns of Billy the Kid, Bat Masterson, and other notables. Altogether he spent a million dollars on his collections. When he showed me the guns he made me stand back a little. He wouldn't let anyone else handle them.

Hart stayed in character to the end. When oil was discovered in the vicinity of his ranch, he refused to allow any drilling on his land. After a number of oil agents had called, he laid up a bull whip and said he would use it on the next to appear. The word went out and he was allowed to remain in peace. His ranch house was on a hill. "It's bad enough to have my view cluttered up with derricks," he told me.

In his last illness, Hart emerged from a coma, saying that he had been on the other side. There he had seen green fields, open ranges, mountains, there had been bright sunlight, and he had heard beautiful music. Then he died.

Even after death he was in character. He had bequeathed his money to the county, saying that the people had given it to him and he was giving it back. His will forbade any drilling for oil on his ranch—though some oil men believe the main pool of the region lies under it.

Bill Hart was an original.

14

THREE years after Mary Pickford came to work for Famous Players in *A Good Little Devil,* her name was a household word all over the land. She was being called "America's Sweetheart"—an understatement. Her popularity was equally high with countless millions in foreign lands.

The first of the great film stars, Mary's rise had been sensational—and more than a little frightening. While preaching a glowing future for motion pictures, I had never prophesied anything like this. Had so wild a vision even come to me—at least that so popular a star would rise so soon—I doubtless would have had my head examined, as people had told me to do.

No one has ever been able to chart the film heavens. We had moved in almost total darkness as Mary led the way upward and across the skies. It takes nothing from her achievement to say that I was always at her side, trying to guide, lend strength—and to guard. If a star could rise so fast—what about the fall?

Other factors besides Mary's personal success were involved. We were building the star system, in which I believed and still believe, and our fortunes were staked on it. Study of the audiences, box-office figures, and fan mail left no doubt that people went to see a player they liked—from whom they expected a certain kind of performance. The exhibitor was pleased by this fact. He was benefiting from the star system. Sight unseen he could book films of Mary Pickford—she was making six or eight a year—and gauge attendance with reasonable accuracy. The same was true of the pictures of Marguerite Clark, William S. Hart, and others. The exhibitor paid a higher rental, of course. The wages of the stars were rising with their fame, and many times faster.

There has never been anything just like the public adulation showered on Mary. It caught us by surprise, but that was nothing to what it did to some others. I recall a Fourth of July when Mary made a personal appearance in Boston. In the evening there was to be an open-air dance, and our publicity men asked the governor to dance with Mary. He agreed with some reluctance. This was before the day any politician was happy to be seen in Mary's presence.

When the governor and Mary went onto the floor most of the other dancers halted. Onlookers pushed in and a circle was formed. Attendants struggled to keep the crowd back. Mary danced demurely, almost shyly, as befitted her curls and her young girl's dress. She seemed unaware of the attention.

The governor believed that all eyes were for him. He

beamed, nodded, and strutted. After the music stopped he graciously allowed Mary to take a bow with him.

In Chicago a dozen policemen were required to break a path for Mary when she left her train. In another city a crowd ripped the top from her taxicab so that she might stand and wave. It was rarely possible for her to go shopping without being recognized. If it happened, her marketing tour was at an end. Many penalties are attached to movie fame, and Mary paid them with good grace, no matter how fatigued. She was truly grateful to her public.

A symbol of her affection was a thing she did without fanfare for a very old lady of our acquaintance. This lady often packed a lunch and spent a whole day at a Mary Pickford film.

When Mary heard about it she decided on a special treat. Donning her girl's dress and letting down her curls, she made an afternoon call. The two had a lovely time and the old lady spoke often of the visit afterwards. I suppose Famous Players could have publicized the incident, but it was a private thing. Mary had done it out of the goodness of her heart and if possible would have done it for every one of her fans.

The public "typed" Mary against her wishes. The sweet ingénue with curls was all right, but she wanted to play a variety of roles. I recall her hard work in *Madame Butterfly*. The art of make-up was crude, and she bought three buckets of mascara to dye her hair, putting the mascara in each morning and washing it out each night.

Curiously, she made up (she applied her own make-up in those days) to seem more like a Japanese girl than the director desired. Mary's forehead was wide, and she fastened the skin of the outer corners of each eye back and achieved the long and slant eyes of the Oriental. The director finally got her to agree to a make-up somewhere nearer the Caucasian.

The public admired Mary's versatility. But it demonstrated conclusively she was wanted complete with curls, puppies, and a jam-smeared face and brave smile while going through some of the worst adversity ever heaped upon a young girl. Reviewers began to speak of a "Mary Pickford role" even when she was not in the picture.

A couple of examples will refresh the memories of the elders while giving the younger generation an idea of what people enjoyed a few decades ago.

In *The Foundling* an artist abandons his baby girl because her birth was responsible for her mother's death. And so at twelve Mary finds herself in a foundling home, where she works hard and is kind to the younger children. This does not save her from abuse by the cruel matron. Finally the artist, stricken with remorse, traces Mary to the foundling home. But the matron has a niece whom she palms off to him as his daughter. Mary is sent to be a slavey in a boardinghouse. There is a happy ending as father and daughter are reunited.

At the beginning of *The Little Princess* Mary is a happy little girl in Bombay. Her father, rich Captain Crewe, about to set out with his best friend to find diamonds, takes Mary to London and leaves her in an exclusive boarding school. Here she makes a friend of Becky, the slavey of the establishment. Word comes that her father is dead in India after having been robbed of everything by his friend, and soon Mary is a slavey, too.

On Christmas Day a neighbor's Indian servant, pursuing his escaped monkey across the roof tops, discovers the two hungry little slaveys in their attic bedroom. His master, a wealthy Englishman, sends the girls a turkey dinner after learning of their plight. He watches across the roofs as the school mistress enters and seizes the food. It turns out that this man is the friend of Mary's father and was actually hastening to him with news of finding a mine worth millions of pounds at the time of Captain Crewe's death. He packs Mary off to a life of luxury, and she does not forget to take along her slavey friend.

Audiences wanted their heroines to be very, very good. There were sirens, true enough. Theodosia Goodman De Coppet, better known as Theda Bara, rose to fame as the vampire in William Fox's *A Fool There Was,* and was the original of the "vamps." In her screen roles Theda Bara was quite as bad as Mary was good.

Mary fretted, but the best we were ever able to do for her was *Stella Maris,* in which she played the dual role of a mean and a sweet girl. It was one of her favorite pictures.

In 1916 Mary was twenty-three, had been married for several years, and was being paid more money than the President of the United States. Yet to the public she was a little girl somewhere between the ages of twelve and eighteen. We did nothing to discourage the illusion.

In Mary's public appearances her mother was always in evidence, but her husband, Owen Moore, hardly ever. I cannot remember, it is true, ever having invited Owen Moore to join the entourage. If the public did not recollect that Mary was a wife, no harm was done. Owen Moore was pleasant and unassuming, and a competent actor. He made pictures for Famous Players and we did everything possible to aid his career. But his name did not creep into Mary's copy.

The two had been drifting apart since their hasty marriage, which was another reason they were not often seen together.

While Mary was not asked to appear in curls and pinafore off the screen, we did, frankly, want her to seem a teen-ager. It was understandable that Mary wished to dress her age and in the height of fashion. But neither of us could afford it. As a customary member of her entourage on personal appearances, I cast an appraising eye, I must confess, on her mode of dress.

Mary liked an occasional drink. For her to take one in public would have been disastrous. Smoking was also taboo. In public—for example in a box at the theater—she could not be permitted to toy with a lipstick, a pencil, or a bit of paper.

From a distance it might be taken for a cigarette. Occasionally she did so thoughtlessly, and I have seen her mother or my wife take the object gently from her fingers.

"If you are to be the queen of motion pictures," I would remind her, "you must pay the penalties of royalty."

Mary liked being queen. One of the best ways of proving top sovereignty was to possess the largest treasury. We startled the film world and the public too, in 1916, by agreeing on a salary of $104,000 a year. And then a group called Mutual hired Charlie Chaplin at just short of $13,000 a week.

Mary felt that her place on the throne was being usurped by a clown—and a relative newcomer at that. There was nothing to do except reopen our salary relations. Under the final terms, Mary was paid $10,000 every Monday. This was an advance against half the profits of a "Mary Pickford Company" organized inside Famous Players. In addition, there was to be a bonus of $300,000 for signing, if and when her pictures earned it.

The total guarantee was $1,040,000 for a two-year period. The million-dollar figure made headlines and Mary felt better for a while.

In the summer of 1916, Famous Players merged with the Jesse L. Lasky Feature Play Company. In a series of talks, Lasky, Goldwyn, De Mille, and I had decided that a combination of our forces was advantageous. There was a slight disagreement between Lasky and me, as the names of our companies indicated. I laid greater emphasis on the star system—that people were mainly drawn to the theaters to see famous players. Lasky contended that the play was the more important. But our debates were always friendly.

It was widely conceded that De Mille, director-general of the Lasky company, was at the head of the production field. The combination of the Lasky and Famous Players studios in Hollywood would be a major step forward in efficiency. In New York, having given up his glove business, Goldwyn was throwing all his dynamic energy into motion pictures.

Although Famous Players was the older and larger, the Lasky company had much to offer and upon my suggestion we divided evenly in the Famous Players-Lasky Corporation, the result of the merger. Goldwyn became chairman of the board, De Mille director-general, Lasky vice-president, and I president.

The new firm's position in the industry was exceptionally strong, though we lacked the financial resources of some others. There was no doubt in my mind that we would strengthen this position and build rapidly on it.

A short time later, owing to an unhappy set of circumstances, I put on my hat and started for the door.

Lasky and I had gotten along fine. He was a creator. Every morning he arrived with a brisk step, full of enthusiasm, loaded with new ideas. The door between our adjoining offices was always open, and by consulting each other constantly we worked smoothly. De Mille made things hum efficiently in Hollywood.

Every hour on the hour, and sometimes the half hour, Sam Goldwyn sent a shock through the organization, in the manner of those pneumatic drills which shake all the buildings in the vicinity. It was Sam's nature. A man of boundless nervous energy, he was always in a terrific hurry, had to keep things whirling in what amounted to a frenzy.

A story told by Harry Reichenbach, the legendary publicity man, of the early days of the Lasky company shows Goldwyn in action. With Lasky still running his vaudeville business and De Mille in Hollywood, Goldwyn was left to run the tiny New York offices. He had a single aid, Reichenbach, and a secretary. Having wound up his glove business, Sam was hard put to keep himself busy. One morning Reichenbach was surprised by two buzzes on a bell which had not been in his office the night before. He sprinted to Goldwyn's office.

Sam announced, "We've got to have efficiency around here. When I buzz once, my secretary comes in with her book. When I buzz twice, you come in."

Reichenbach, a man of no reverence, bided his time until the next morning, when he appeared with an electrician. They switched the buzzer apparatus. Now the button was in Reichenbach's office, the bell in Goldwyn's. Sam arrived, Reichenbach pressed the button. Goldwyn sprinted to *his* office.

"That's efficiency," Reichenbach said, "the way you said."

Goldwyn laughed and agreed that the time was not yet ripe for a buzzer system.

Before long I was convinced that Goldwyn disagreed many times only for the sake of argument. It is no disservice to him to say that he liked operating in a turmoil, inasmuch as in the nearly forty years since that time he has become celebrated for it. But I liked to move with greater care. My aim was the building of a large and wide-flung organization, while he operated in the moment.

Sam was not a believer, one might say, in parliamentary procedure. A chairman of the board does not ordinarily concern himself with the day-to-day details of operation. Sam did, and by temperament he had to, though I didn't know it at the time. One day, for example, I had just completed a contract with Jack Pickford, Mary's brother, calling for five hundred dollars a week. Sam canceled it, saying the figure was too high. His post didn't give him authority to do that. But, as I say, rules meant little to Sam when he was excited.

And so within a few months I knew that one of us was out of water in Famous Players-Lasky. The decision did not come easy. It is true that when confronted with a problem I always took to the streets and walked. For that matter, I walked five or six miles every day—nearly always to and from the Switzerland Apartments at Riverside Drive and 156th Street to which we had moved.

Faced with this problem, I would find myself late at night down at the Battery and then, seemingly a few minutes later, entering Central Park, miles uptown. In the end I decided to put the solution in more objective hands, those of Lasky and De Mille. If they believed that the chances for Famous Players-Lasky was better with me gone, I would depart without rancor. I was perfectly confident of my ability to start over again.

The matter came to a head while Lasky was discussing Mary Pickford's next film with her. They held their conferences in our combination library and board room. Goldwyn kept dashing in with suggestions and exiting with door slamming.

One evening after Goldwyn and Mary had both departed, I walked into the library.

"Jesse," I said, "I have come to an unhappy conclusion which may distress you more than it does me. It is a hard thing to ask you to choose between your brother-in-law and me. But many a film company has failed because of internal dissention, and I can see it happening with us. The decision will rest with you and De Mille. You do what you think best and I will go my way, whichever you choose, without a bitter thought."

I communicated the same thought to De Mille and he came on from the west coast. They asked me to stay. Goldwyn had no hard feelings, nor did I. We had several conversations and agreed that our temperaments and methods were too different for things to continue the way they had been. A division of stock was arranged and Goldwyn's share, which we purchased, came to a little under a million dollars—a neat enough sum for four years in the picture business.

Afterwards Goldwyn joined with the Selwyns and later was a part of Metro-Goldwyn-Mayer. After departing from that organization he became an independent producer, concentrating his enormous energies brilliantly on a picture or two at a time, and gained his deservedly eminent place in the film world.

Not long after the Famous Players-Lasky crisis, the differences inside the distributing organization, Paramount Pictures Corporation, came to a boil, and I was selected to head it. Paramount was to remain a distributing agency, handling the films of other companies as well as those of Famous Players-Lasky.

There is no set of figures which quickly illustrates how enormously the film industry had grown during the four years since Famous Players' introduction of feature pictures. Perhaps I can give a rough idea by noting that I had opened conversations with Otto Kahn, head of the great banking firm of Kuhn, Loeb & Company, for a loan of ten million dollars. My associates held that the request for so large a sum was preposterous. I pointed out that if we got it, motion pictures would be regarded as an important industry. A request for only five million dollars, I argued, might be rejected by Kuhn, Loeb & Company on the ground that the firm dealt only in larger sums.

Besides a great financier, Otto Kahn was a patron of the arts, notably as head of the Metropolitan Opera. Consequently, I approached him with a double argument. I pointed out that the screen was becoming the entertainment medium of the great body of the public. Sufficient working capital would allow us to improve both pictures and theaters, adding to the pleasure of wide audiences. At the same time, I argued, we were an excellent financial risk, being the spearhead of a vast new industry. Kuhn, Loeb & Company helped us with a stock issue of ten million dollars.

15

EVERYBODY knows that Mary Pickford married Douglas Fairbanks and that for many years they reigned as king and queen of Hollywood. It was a royal courtship, and it put gray hairs in my head. I will speak a little of it to show one more facet of the moviemaker's varied existence—his need to concern himself even with the noblest of romances to avoid the merest breath of public scandal. But first let me discuss Fairbanks, the most popular leading man of his time and perhaps of any other. His career sheds much light on the making of a great screen star.

It will be noticed that I speak little of the "discovery" of a star. If a producer uses a player as an extra or for a bit part, and that player later becomes famous, the producer sometimes claims discovery. That is nonsense. Suppose the producer realizes the potentialities of such a player and conscientiously tries to build him. Here the producer is entitled to some credit. But he tries with a hundred where he succeeds with one.

Stardom is a matter over which only audiences have any real control. Something in a player's personality which they like is transmitted via the screen. Naturally, a woman's beauty or a man's handsome countenance is an asset. So is acting technique—though we learned soon enough that many excellent stage players failed to make contact, as it were, with the movie audience.

It is true that we can anticipate to some degree the response by means of auditions and screen tests. A player of "star material" may be tried in various small parts while we analyze the reactions. If the audiences take to him, then we can do much to help by supplying proper roles and publicity. Many times the audiences surprise us by choosing a player we had not thought of as star material. We try to figure out why, and proceed accordingly.

After trying with thousands, and working with scores of stars as they have risen and faded, I have arrived at two conclusions. One is that the star who lasts must have a very strong character—even if that character is not altogether admirable off the screen. The other is that the lasting popular star always plays himself or herself, or a part thereof.

There is no better illustration of the points I am making than Fairbanks. On the stage he had been only fairly successful as a light comedian. In his immensely popular pictures he was romantic, athletic, full of clean fun, and a bit of a show-off—Douglas Fairbanks in the flesh.

Doug was the son of H. Charles Ulman, a New York attorney. Later his mother divorced Ulman and resumed the name of Fairbanks, that of her first husband. Doug adopted it long before he was an actor. In his late teens he appeared in a few stage roles. But, always restless, he got a job as order clerk in Wall Street with the idea of becoming a king of finance.

Failing to achieve equality with J. P. Morgan at once, he shifted to a hardware firm, went on a bumming tour of Europe after crossing on a cattle boat, studied law briefly, worked in a tool machine factory, and finally wound up as a Broadway actor under the management of Bill Brady. For the next thirteen years he was a professional stage player and an amateur boxer, wrestler, horseman, gymnast, and practical joker.

Doug was thirty-one when, in 1915, he went to Hollywood in a grab bag of sixty stage players gathered by the newly formed Triangle Company. Neither Triangle nor many of the others lasted. Given more attention, Doug might not have either. D. W. Griffith, who had been hired as Triangle's top director, after observing Doug's chair handstands, leaps, and assorted other playful shenanigans on the sets, advised him to apply for work in Keystone Comedies.

Griffith turned Doug over to his assistant, Frank Woods, who passed him on to director John Emerson and scenarist Anita Loos, still in her teens, to see if anything could be done. What they did, in effect, was to turn the camera on him in the midst of his good-natured horseplay. Audiences responded favorably and he was on his way.

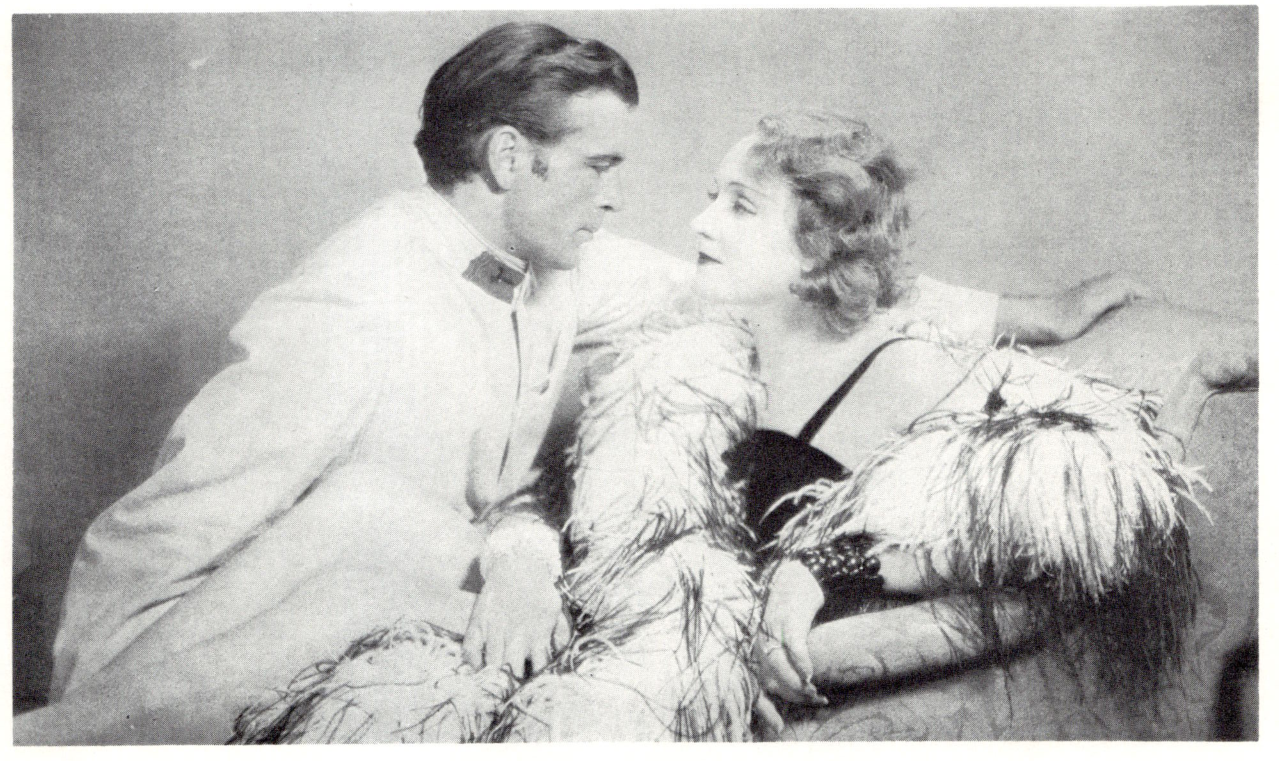

Gary Cooper and Marlene Dietrich in *Morocco* (1930).

The Zukors go to the movies.

Gloria Swanson and Adolph Zukor (1952).

Rosemary Clooney looks on as Mr. Zukor makes his handprint at Grauman's Chinese Theatre (Hollywood, 1953).

Not long afterward our company made arrangements with Fairbanks for him to make his own pictures with our help and our marketing. Thus Doug and I became acquainted in a business way and soon were friends. He was wonderful—if rather strenuous—company.

I recall an afternoon when, had a camera been handy, I could have shot a few reels that would have provided screen entertainment for millions. This was some time later, but I will jump ahead for a moment because the incident is a perfect illustration of Fairbanks the individual.

I stopped by the Fairbanks set—he was shooting *The Mark of Zorro*—intending to have a chat with him. Sometime during the morning, I learned, he had stopped production and had gone home. His assistants were distressed, because a mob scene was being shot and the cost of stopping was heavy.

I drove on to Doug's house.

"Mr. Fairbanks is swimming," a butler informed me.

I set off across the rolling lawn, though the pool's edge was deserted. The water surface did not become visible until I was near at hand. It was unbroken. Reasoning that Fairbanks had gone back to the house without the butler's knowledge, I prepared to turn away.

Suddenly a head popped to the surface. I knew the broad sunburned face very well, but I was no less flabbergasted than if it had belonged to the King of England.

It was Babe Ruth.

Another head popped up—that of Walter Johnson, the celebrated pitcher.

Up popped number three. Al Kaufman.

Last of all came Doug.

I sank into a chair, feeling slightly faint, as they scrambled out. While they sunned themselves and talked I was able to piece the story together. These big happy boys had been playing follow-the-leader. My arrival had coincided with a trial to see who could stay under water the longest. Doug, the leader of the moment—and I suspected most of the rest of the time—had won.

The baseball stars were in Los Angeles for a benefit show that Al was managing. Al had taken them to see Fairbanks. After finishing a scene or two, Doug had dismissed the cast for the day. To the objections of his assistants he replied that nothing could be allowed to stand in the way of an afternoon with his sports heroes.

I clapped my hand to my forehead, thankful that he was footing that budget, not me, and the cost of time wasted would come out of his profits.

The conversation at the pool's edge was interrupted by the butler, serving, as it were, Babe Ruth's uniform. Doug had prevailed upon the slugger to send to his hotel for it.

There was never any doubt in my mind who was going to wear the uniform on this particular afternoon. Doug was into it in a flash. One or two more of us could have got in, too.

Another servant arrived with a couple of bats, some gloves, and three or four boxes of baseballs which Doug had sent for. I expected home plate and the bases to arrive at any moment.

Doug said to Walter Johnson, "Mind pitching a few to me?"

"Happy to," Johnson replied.

Fairbanks knew that I was an old catcher, and he offered me the post. But I declined to try to hold the greatest fireball pitcher of his time.

Johnson grooved a few, but with plenty of steam, and Doug hit them pretty well. He was a fine athlete with beautiful co-ordination.

"Babe," Doug said after a while, "mind if I pitch you a few?"

The home-run champion grinned. "Let's go."

He picked up a bat and took his famous stance.

"Now really try," Doug said. "Don't be polite."

But Ruth was, for a couple of pitches. Then he connected with a terrific line drive. It was a foul—headed straight for Fairbanks' mansion. I looked at Doug. His face was alight with happiness. Then a shadow crossed it as the ball struck the side of the house. I knew that he had been hoping for a window.

Unfortunately, I had to excuse myself to keep an appointment. Departing, I saw a servant firing up a barbecue contraption. Everybody knew that Babe Ruth liked hot dogs. Doug was not the host to disappoint him.

In the day house of my summer home we had a big swing which hung from the rafters by chains. Usually we ate in the day house. While others relaxed after the meal over coffee, Doug, when a guest, would go hand-over-hand up one of the chains and do stunts on the rafters.

While on a train to Hollywood one time I glanced up from a card game to see Doug kibitzing—from outside the window. His face expressed disapproval of the way I was playing my cards. My own face doubtless registered greater concern for his safety, for the train was going at a fast pace.

He liked to do imitations. Probably his best was Sam Goldwyn in a fury, which gave him an opportunity to pop in and out of doors, slam them, and to use some of Sam's colorful phrasing. As for myself, I never noticed that Sam used malapropisms as a general thing, though he got a reputation for doing so. Doug claimed to have heard him shout, "An oral contract is not worth the paper it's written on."

In the later years of his film career, Fairbanks went in for swashbuckling costume pieces such as *The Three Musketeers, The Thief of Bagdad,* and *The Black Pirate.* I have always thought his better films were the early ones in which he portrayed a laughing, high-spirited, athletic American male—exaggerated yet true to type. Doug was a homespun philosopher of a sort, author of *Whistle and Hoe—Sing as We Go* and similar books. His idea was to cheer people up by his movies as well as by his real-life antics.

A good example of his early themes was *Reaching for the Moon,* made for us in 1917. Doug plays the role of Alexis Caesar Napoleon Brown, a young man of soaring ambitions employed in a button factory. In his spare time, and some of the company's, he studies New Thought, a system teaching that heavy concentration on a desired goal will win it. Doug wants a life of fame and glamor, whereas his girl Elsie dreams of a cottage for the two. She dutifully studies a book on New Thought, but when Doug is fired for daydreaming she advises him to quit "reaching for the moon."

It develops that Doug is heir to the throne of a small European kingdom and he sets off to mount it. Being a king is not quite as pleasant as he had expected. A gang of cutthroats tries to assassinate him, a situation permitting Doug to fight, leap, swim, and perform other athletic feats. His more sensational clashes were with his old wrestling trainer, gigantic Bull Montana, whom he had brought to Hollywood. After Doug is stabbed, blown up by a bomb, thrown into a canal, and almost betrothed to an ugly princess of a nearby kingdom, he rushes to Elsie and the button factory.

One night in the now happily married couple's cottage, Elsie is reading in the concentration book. Doug wants to throw it into the fire. Elsie says no, she has become a convert, for powerful concentration on her twin goals of marriage to him and the cottage have brought them to pass. Doug agrees that concentration is all right as long as one does not "reach for the moon."

That was Doug's best formula—plenty of action and homey common sense.

About the time of *Reaching for the Moon,* a rumor came to me that Doug was in the habit of telephoning Mary Pickford fairly often and dropping in for a chat.

Now, there was nothing wrong about these two being

friends, even romantically inclined toward one another. Mary had been living apart from Owen Moore for some time. Their marriage was over except in name. Doug was married and had a young son, Douglas, Jr. I understood that he was estranged from his wife. Mary, at least, had talked of divorce. But that was not simple.

The queen does not suddenly get divorced—especially if a large body of her subjects does not even know that she is married. Like many a royal lady before her, Mary chafed at her bonds. She was very tired of her eternal little-girl role on the screen and in public. Here was a vigorous, blooming young lady in her middle twenties, a millionairess two times over by her own efforts, courageous—even willful. Though plenty of "Little Mary" remained, she wanted to be her whole self before the world, as well as to play more mature roles on the screen.

I was convinced that the public, no matter how much we helped, would not accept a quick change from "Little Mary" to a young woman of the world. Mary and I had argued endlessly over making *A Poor Little Rich Girl,* with her protesting that at last she was too old for the role of teen-ager. In the end I won that argument and the picture was a great hit. But its success only proved the strength of the bonds which tied Mary to her public role. She chafed more than ever.

As soon as I heard the rumors about Doug and Mary, I went to see her mother. She was aware of the situation.

"Yes," she said. "Mary is quite fond of Douglas."

In my mind there was a companion thought—how fond of Mary is Doug? It occurred to me that the mere paying of court to the queen might appeal to his romantic nature.

"The smallest breath of scandal can ruin Mary's career," I said. "Fairbanks will survive. After all, nothing really bad is happening, or is going to happen between them. The public will forgive a dashing fellow like Doug. But it has taken Mary to its heart in a different way. As the sweet daughter or sister much more is expected of her. If Mary appears to fail the public's trust, it will punish her."

Charlotte nodded. "I've told Mary so."

Neither of us had forgotten that Mary had disobeyed her mother by eloping with Owen Moore. If Mary was in love with Doug, and he was in love with her, we knew that she would marry him no matter if it smashed her career beyond repair. It is ironical, I suppose, that Mary could not portray on the screen the indomitable woman who was one part of her.

If Mary and Doug were serious about each other, it was up to Charlotte Pickford and me to do our level best to prevent a smashup of Mary's career.

"Well," I said, rising to go, "I'll have to make inquiries as to whether the intentions of the gentleman are honorable."

Mrs. Pickford laughed. "Will you ask him?"

"Oh, no. Doubtless he would turn three or four cartwheels, shinny up the waterspout, leap from the roof to a tree, do a double back-flip to the ground, and I might not hear enough of his answer to satisfy me."

It is never pleasant to interfere with the lives of others.

But the sad truth is that movie producers occasionally have to. This can be regarded, I suppose, as a cynical matter of business. We spend hundreds of thousands of dollars in building a star and often millions more are wrapped up in pictures awaiting release. Naturally we think of those things—as well as possible harm to the entire industry.

But a major film producer must concern himself also with the human elements, or he doesn't last long. Many a star, temporarily overwrought, is unable to clearly judge the public's reaction to a given incident. We therefore often talk in a straightforward but sympathetic way to a player about his or her behavior. I am frank in saying that we take character—for example emotional balance—into account before going all out in star building.

Mary and Doug were beginning to see a good deal of each other. When not together, they telephoned. I couldn't hold a conversation with Mary but that Fairbanks interrupted it with a call. They were very discreet, or thought they were. In New York they sometimes donned motorist's linen dusters and goggles and drove about, believing themselves disguised. It was the sort of thing that appealed especially to Doug's romanticism.

My reason for not discussing the subject with Fairbanks was simply that I would not have been convinced by anything he said. Not that he lacked honesty. I simply had no way of being sure of what went on under his exuberant exterior. It occurred to me that he might have convinced himself that he was sure of his feeling for Mary, while deep down he was not at all.

The person to know best was Mary, and finally I tackled the subject with her. We had dinner at a quiet place and I began by mentioning the talk inside the trade.

"The point has been reached," I said, "that some little incident will occur—maybe that automobile will break down and a reporter will happen along and penetrate your disguise. The dam will break. What if, to put the worst face on it, Owen Moore sues for divorce, naming Fairbanks as correspondent? Or his wife sues him, naming you? Above all—are you very, very sure about your feelings?"

Mary's blue eyes were graver than I had even seen them. "I am sure," she said simply.

I knew that she was. "And Fairbanks?"

Mary nodded. "Equally. I know."

"All right," I said. "That part is settled. Now what about the public?"

Here we disagreed.

"The public will understand," Mary said. "We are in love and we are sincere and the public will not deny us our happiness."

"That could well be," I said, "if you are able to sit down with every member of the audience as you do with me. But what if the public gets a bad account? Flaunt the public—even appear to—and it will make you answer."

The indomitable spirit which had carried Mary to the top showed in her face. "Whatever the price, we'll carry through. Not that we won't do everything possible to avoid bad publicity. There will be no flaunting."

And so that was the way it was going to be. Three long years were to pass before the royal wedding was possible. In-between there were explosions, but they were kept muffled. At one point Owen Moore stated publicly that he intended to proceed legally against Fairbanks, who was the first to get a divorce. But Moore did nothing and said no more. Finally a divorce was arranged by Mary and Moore in Nevada, after which the Nevada attorney general accused them of collusion and fraud. Charges were not pressed and shortly thereafter—in March of 1920—Mary and Fairbanks were married at last.

By this time Mary and I had come to a parting of business ways.

The first shot had been fired in what movie chroniclers describe as a major "war" of the industry in 1917. Historian Terry Ramsaye remarks that at the time "Zukor was busy counting all the jewels of starland into the box of the Famous Players-Lasky Corporation."

We had a galaxy of them, all right. At the top were Mary, Doug, Bill Hart, and Marguerite Clark. Shining almost as brightly—and some of whom were to shine brighter still—were Pauline Frederick, Wallace Reid, John Barrymore, Ann Pennington, Billie Burke, Charles Ray, Vivian Martin, Fannie Ward, George M. Cohan, Geraldine Farrar, Jack Pickford, Louise Huff, Dorothy Dalton, Lou Tellegen, Elsie Ferguson, Julian Eltinge, Sessue Hayakawa, Enid Bennett, and Mae Murray.

The aforementioned shot was fired by the exhibitors under the general leadership of Tom Tally of Los Angeles and my old penny arcade partner, Mitchell Mark of New York City. The First National Exhibitors' Circuit was formed with the announced intention of invading the picture production field. The exhibitors argued that the rental cost of big-star films was too high. I answered that the price of the stars was very high.

The First National group promptly sent the price skyrocketing with a daring raid on the major players. In self-defense, our company began to buy theaters, including strings of them. The battle commenced to wax hot.

The initial prize captured by the exhibitors group was Charlie Chaplin. They agreed to pay him $1,070,000 for eight two-reel pictures. Next they offered Mary Pickford $1,050,000 for three feature pictures.

Mary's contract with Famous Players-Lasky ran out in the spring of 1918. Those five years since *A Good Little Devil* had constituted an epoch in movie history, but neither Mary nor I had changed very much. She told me frankly of the offer, as she had of those before.

"Mary," I said, "it is too big this time. It wouldn't be sound business to pay you what you would want to stay with us."

She was silent for a moment. "I'm sorry," she said. "I'm very sorry."

"Well," I said, "we have nothing to complain about, you and I."

She smiled. "No. We've done the best we could for each other."

Mary stayed with First National for only a few months, and then, in the spring of 1919, joined Fairbanks, Chaplin, and D. W. Griffith in organizing United Artists. The original plan called for William S. Hart as a fifth party. In the end he stayed with Famous Players-Lasky, kindly giving as his reason his friendship with me.

I will now take leave of Mary, so far as this narrative is concerned. At the climax of the Hollywood banquet celebrating my eightieth birthday, the stage curtains opened without announcement. There stood Mary, dressed in white, looking a score of years younger than her sixty. In a warm and nostalgic address she expressed regret at ever having left my "sheltering arm."

Whether her future career might have been any different is more than I or anyone else can say. The public's taste changed and the ingénue was out of style long before Mary's retirement—honored and with her fortune intact—a decade later. I was saddened that her marriage to Fairbanks broke up after fifteen years. But her happiness was restored with her marriage to Charles Rogers—known more widely as Buddy when he played for us. She remains the gallant, warmhearted Mary I have always known.

16

NOW let us hurry back to the turbulent, boiling Hollywood of the late teens and early twenties. Most of Hollywood's people had come from humble beginnings. They had never expected to have much money—yet here they were, rolling in it. Having struck it rich without knowing exactly how or why, they could not get it through their heads that the gold might peter out.

Take for example a young actor or actress who a couple of years earlier had been making twenty-five or thirty dollars a week as a clerk, or the same amount in stock. He or she might now be collecting five hundred to a thousand dollars a week, more than the richest man in the old home town. Yet it was a rare performer who did not feel underpaid.

Suppose a girl made a small hit in a film—perhaps because the role fit her exactly. A producer, seeing her, asked at once, "Have you a contract? If you have, can you break it?" If she signed with him she would become dissatisfied immediately. Another producer was sure to be along soon with a bigger offer. The stronger her contract, the more fabulous the offer—and the greater the player's dissatisfaction.

The town was full of irresponsible agents, who reminded me of gamblers and confidence men in a gold rush camp. They walked around, representing nobody, and made fantastic promises. To a player getting five hundred dollars a week, an agent would say, "If you were free, I could get you two thousand dollars." Gold nuggets were lying about in such abundance that even this type of agent was able to pick up enough to give him a flashy living.

Strike-it-rich people have a tendency to spend their money on lavish display and high living, including dissipation, and the inhabitants of the movie colony followed the pattern. We had our troubles getting the players to the studio and made up by nine o'clock, when the cameras began turning. Many had to be telephoned or sent after. We cautioned endlessly that good health was essential, for the camera is merciless. The best make-up artist cannot altogether hide tired or dissipated lines. Sometimes we had to lay off a company for a day to permit a leading player to rest. Though expensive, it was cheaper than a bad appearance on the screen.

Some, like Tommy Meighan, had their personal problems but did their level best to overcome them. Tommy, enormously popular in tough he-man roles, was fine and gentle, perhaps one of the stars closest to my family. But he was a periodical drinker. When time came to make a picture he set his glass down and did not take another drop until it was finished. Then some little thing would happen and seemingly for no reason he began to drink again. It was a worrisome thing for him and for us. But he was a mature, sincere man fighting to do his best. And because he was charitable and obliging—under a gruff outer surface—he was always an asset to the industry.

One could not help but sympathize with Wallace Reid, a big, likable fellow who photographed much slimmer than his 180 pounds. Wally may have had too much money for his own good, for he was a thrill seeker—though not in conquest of women, fascinated as they were with him. One time while making a picture in New York he was pursued by two or three beautiful stage stars. Wally paid no attention. He was married to Dorothy Davenport, a screen star, and the high point of his evening was a telephone call to her in California.

Wally was a great lover of the outdoors. He liked to hunt and fish and, above all, to race automobiles. He lived his life to the hilt. Perhaps excitement overtaxed his nerves, or, as was widely reported, he may have tried one too many thrills. In any event, the narcotics habit got a hold on him. We sent him away for rests and hired masseurs to work on him between brief appearances before the camera.

But gradually he declined and died at the age of thirty. The fact of his addiction was widely known—his wife founded a sanitarium to help those in similar trouble—and many people jumped to the conclusion that dope taking was common in Hollywood.

Charles Ray was an example of the player who overestimated his talent and lived on the scale of a potentate while his head swelled far above its normal size. His palatial home was celebrated for its enormous turquoise bathtub, its fifteen-thousand-dollar dining-room table, and its liveried servants. The press carried reports that his wife never wore the same gown twice.

Curiously, Ray was a great success only in country bumpkin roles. He had come from the small Illinois town of Jacksonville, entering the movies as extra after a brief period in smalltime musicals and vaudeville. His soft big-eyed face was almost pretty rather than handsome.

Typical of his pictures was *The Egg Crate Wallop,* with Colleen Moore. In it he was a wrestler of egg crates and other packages for an express company in a hick town. Colleen, daughter of the express agent, was soda jerker in the local drugstore. A city slicker, a prize fighter of talent, came along and made a play for Colleen, besides stealing a bundle of money from the express company's safe and pinning the blame on the hero. While in the big city on the lam, Ray tried his hand at prize fighting, was matched with the slicker, and laid him low with his "egg crate wallop."

We tried Ray as other types, but the country boy was the only one he could play. Nevertheless his pictures did well and it seemed to us that he had a few years to go before the public tired of him. It fell to my lot, as in the case with so many others, to endeavor to tell him the facts of movie life.

He came to my office and, as was my custom, I suggested that we look at the books.

He was not interested.

"But," I argued, "you are making four pictures a year and from taking the figures on a set of those we can get an average which will demonstrate your value to us."

"No, thank you," he answered politely. "I'm interested only in the salary you are prepared to offer."

"Mr. Ray," I continued sympathetically, "you aren't really a leading-man type. You can never be the romantic figure who commands a top salary. You play the farmer come to town, and you do it well. We want you to keep on playing that character and we will pay you the highest price we can."

He waited.

"A quarter of a million dollars a year," I said. "Five thousand a week."

His brown eyes grew larger and I thought the deal was set. I was mistaken.

"Mr. Zukor," he said, "that offer is an insult."

I quit right there, and I must say that I felt somewhat as a man who had intended to bet on a horse but failed to get his money down and it came in loser. Here was an actor who had so far overestimated himself as to lose touch with reality. I knew he was headed for trouble and did not care to be with him when he found it.

Ray had the courage of his convictions. After trying elsewhere he financed his own pictures. But he slipped downhill until finally he was playing bit roles.

Picture stars were coming more and more into the public eye. Fan magazines had sprung up and every day the newspapers devoted columnar miles of space to film subjects. This was to the good. We co-operated by furnishing copy, raising the shades, so to speak, for the public to look at us. Therefore we had no right to complain if some people didn't like what they saw. Many held that film salaries were too high, that riches led to overworldliness and inevitably to sin.

The postwar revolution of manners and morals had set in. The flapper was making her appearance. Skirts were going up. The younger generation evidently was hell-bent on emancipation. Their elders watched this revolution aghast.

The film industry was caught in the middle. Our prime aim, as I remarked earlier, is always to keep abreast of audience taste and ahead if possible. And the moviegoers were mainly young people, as they are today. Consequently film subject matter was changing to fit the times.

One of our major successes in 1920, for example, was Cecil B. De Mille's *Male and Female,* starring Thomas Meighan and Gloria Swanson, and featuring Bebe Daniels, Raymond Hatton, and Lila Lee. Based on J. M. Barrie's stage play *The Admirable Crichton,* it depicted a noble English family, complete with servants, shipwrecked in a wild and lonely place—with lions and some Oriental touches which had not been in the play. The story dealt mainly with the rise of the party's strongest male, the butler, to dominance because of his ability to cope with adverse circumstances.

It was a highly moral picture, yet its emotional theme —the noble lady falling in love with the butler—would probably not have been acceptable to prewar audiences.

Meanwhile several fly-by-night companies were producing quickies which went far over the line of good taste. This, coupled with objection to new themes and the moral revolution in general, brought a clamor for film censorship. We had narrowly averted federal censorship back in 1916 with the formation of the National Association of the Motion Picture Industry, and had been able to keep our house in order for a number of years. With fourteen thousand theaters selling fifty million tickets a week, the industry was plainly obligated to show decent pictures. But federal or state censorship was not the proper answer, in our opinion, and we began looking around for a better one.

An event in the early fall of 1921 hastened our search. At a party in a San Francisco hotel a minor screen actress named Virginia Rappe died under mysterious circumstances. The blame was placed on Fatty Arbuckle and he was arrested. The press reports of a drinking party were unsavory, and the rumors were far worse. Arbuckle was eventually acquitted. But that did little to abate the tornado of criticism which descended on the whole film industry.

Our company had several Arbuckle comedies ready for release. To have shown them might have resulted in riots, had exhibitors been willing to try. At best the outcry would be so great as to damage the whole industry. We laid them away at a loss of roughly a million dollars and they have never been released. Later Arbuckle worked as a director, using an alias, but to the day of his death in 1933 the storm had not abated sufficiently so that he could make another picture.

After Arbuckle's arrest the industry leaders moved quickly to organize ourselves into the Motion Picture Producers and Distributors of America. The main purpose was to formulate a written code for guidance in film subject matter. An unwritten code of behavior for industry personnel was contemplated as well.

As the man best qualified to administer it, we agreed on slender, affable Will H. Hays, then Postmaster General, and signed a round-robin request for him to serve. He had accepted but was not yet in his post when another major scandal rocked the industry.

William Desmond Taylor, a director for us and other companies, was a handsome, sophisticated man of forty-five. We knew little of his past except that since 1912 he had been a film actor and director. One night somebody entered his house and shot him dead.

His real name, it came out, was William Cunningham Deane-Tanner, born in Ireland, a former rancher in the American West, and New York City antique dealer. One day in 1908, Deane-Tanner had disappeared from his shop. His wife, who had divorced him, and his daughter recognized him four years later on the screen.

In Hollywood Taylor's valet and chauffeur, a mysterious fellow called Sands, had forged his employer's name to a number of checks and then had disappeared. He was never located. A doubly curious twist to this strange case was that a brother of Taylor's had dropped out of sight in much the same way as he had. Many people believed Sands to be this missing brother.

The murder of any screen director would have brought enough bad publicity. Taylor's strange career compounded the trouble and, in addition, the names of other screen notables were drawn into the case. Mabel Normand had dropped by Taylor's house on the evening of the murder to pick up some books he had bought for her. Witnesses had seen Taylor escorting Mabel to her automobile, and she was not suspected. But her name increased the size of the headlines.

It developed, too, that blonde little Mary Miles Minter, a teen-age ingénue in the Mary Pickford tradition, had been secretly engaged to Taylor. After learning of the tragedy, she had rushed to his home and made a hysterical scene. Headlines and more headlines.

Dope was dragged into the case because Taylor was campaigning against the traffic. Authorities considered the possibility that underworld figures had slain him. Whatever the true facts, they have never been brought to light. As mysteries go, the Taylor case was good reading and newspapers sent dozens of special correspondents who described Hollywood as a wicked, wicked city.

Thus the seas upon which Will Hays embarked were exceedingly rough. From the beginning he negotiated them with skill. Later he was tagged as a "czar" by the press. Nothing could have been further from the truth. He was a consummate diplomat and his keen judgment and tireless efforts were of great importance to the industry.

17

LATE in 1921 our advertising copywriters took off their gloves, spit on their hands, and hammered out some remarkable advice to the public.

SEE:

—the auction of beautiful girls to the lords of Algerian harems.

—the barbaric gambling fete in the glittering Casino of Biskra.

—the heroine, disguised, invade the Bedouins' secret slave rites.

—Sheik Ahmed raid her caravan and carry her off to his tent.

—her stampede his Arabian horses and dash away to freedom.

—her captured by bandit tribesmen and enslaved by their chief in his stronghold.

—the fierce battle of Ahmed's clans to rescue the girl from his foes.

—the Sheik's vengeance, the storm in the desert, a proud woman's heart surrendered.

—matchless scenes of gorgeous color, and wild free life, and love. In the year's supreme screen thrill—

By this time all readers over forty, and doubtless most of those under, will have guessed the rest. The picture was, of course, *The Sheik,* with Rudolph Valentino.

Top billing went not to Valentino but to the leading lady, Agnes Ayres. Valentino was twenty-six years old and had been in Hollywood for several years, dancing as a professional partner and sometimes playing bit movie parts, chiefly as a villain. Recently he had gained attention as a tango-dancing Argentine in *The Four Horsemen of the Apocalypse,* made by another company. When we hired him for *The Sheik* we expected that he would perform satisfactorily, but little more. We certainly did not expect him to convulse the nation.

Valentino was as strange a man as I ever met. Before going into his personality, however, it would seem worthwhile, taking into account what happened afterward, to review *The Sheik.*

The story was taken from a novel of the same title by Edith M. Hull, an Englishwoman. After publication abroad the book had become a sensational best seller in America. We paid fifty thousand dollars for the screen rights, a very large sum for the time, with the idea that the novel's popularity would assure the picture's success.

The story gets under way with Diana Mayo (Agnes Ayres), a haughty English girl visiting in Biskra, remarking that marriage is captivity. Since Diana is a willful, adventurous girl who dislikes the restraining hand of her cautious brother, one knows that trouble is brewing the moment she spots Sheik Ahmed Ben Hassan (Valentino) and their eyes meet. The distance between them is roughly 150 feet, yet she quails, to use understatement, visibly. One might have thought he had hit her on the head with a thrown rock. There was nothing subtle about film emotion in those days.

Learning that non-Arabs are forbidden at the fete the Sheik is holding in the Biskra casino that night, Diana disguises herself as a slave girl and wins admission. The Sheik discovers her identity as she is about to be auctioned off along with other slaves. He allows her to escape, but later that night appears under her window, singing:

> "I'm the Sheik of Araby
> Your love belongs to me.
> At night when you're asleep
> Into your tent I creep."

Valentino moved his lips hardly at all when he sang. As a matter of fact, his acting was largely confined to protruding his large, almost occult, eyes until vast areas of white were visible, drawing back the lips of his wide, sensuous mouth to bare his gleaming teeth, and flaring his nostrils.

But to get on with the film story. Next day the Sheik attacks Diana's caravan and packs her off to his desert oasis camp. Though he regards her as his bride, she fends off his advances. Yet it is soon apparent that she is falling in love with him. After a week of virtual slavery Diana begins to like it at the camp.

Then she learns that Raoul de Saint Hubert, a French author and friend of the Sheik, is coming to visit. Ashamed to be found in her slavelike condition by a fellow European, Diana stampedes her guard's horse while riding in the desert and makes a dash for freedom. Her horse breaks a leg and she staggers across the sand toward a distant caravan.

This is the caravan of the dread bandit Omair (played by Walter Long, a noted heavy). Omair makes her a captive for plainly evil reasons. But soon the Sheik, having been informed of Diana's escape by the stampeded guard, attacks the caravan and rescues her.

The French author (Adolph Menjou, wearing a bushier mustache than was his custom in later years) rebukes the Sheik for what seems to him a selfish attitude toward the girl. Next day while Diana and the Frenchman are riding in the desert, Omair swoops down, wounds the author, and carries the girl off to his stronghold.

The Sheik gathers his horsemen and rides to the rescue.

Meanwhile at the stronghold, Omair pursues the "white gazelle," as he calls Diana, around and around a room in his harem house. One of the bandit's wives, fed up with him, has advised Diana to commit suicide rather than become the brute's victim. But Diana, having faith in the Sheik, fights gamely on.

The Sheik and his horsemen assault the stronghold's walls. Once inside, the Sheik bests Omair in a hand-to-hand struggle. But at the moment of victory a huge slave hits him a terrible blow on the head.

For some days he lies at death's door.

Now the Frenchman tells Diana the true story of the Sheik. He is no Arab at all, but of English and Spanish descent. When a baby he was abandoned in the desert. An old sheik found him, reared him, had him educated in France, and eventually left him in command of the tribe.

And so the story draws to a happy ending. The Sheik recovers and the two lovers set off for civilization and marriage.

The public, especially the women, mobbed the theaters, and it was not very long before the psychologists were busying themselves with explanations. The simplest, I gathered, was that a surprisingly large number of American women wanted a mounted sheik to carry them into the desert. Doubtless for only a short stay, as in the case of Diana, after which they would be returned to civilization in style.

Adult males were inclined to regard *The Sheik* with some levity. But the youths began to model themselves on Valentino, especially after he had appeared in *Blood and Sand* for us. In the latter picture, playing a Spanish bullfighter, he affected sideburns, sleek hair, and wide-bottomed trousers. Soon thousands of boys and young men had cultivated sideburns, allowed their hair to grow long, plastered it down, and were wearing bell-bottomed pants. Lads in this getup were called "sheiks." Thus two of Valentino's roles were combined to get a young modern sheik.

An audience today viewing *The Sheik* laughs at the melodramatic story, the exaggerated gestures, and Valentino's wild-eyed stares and heaving panting while demonstrating his affection for Diana. Yet some of the impact of his personality remains. He created an atmosphere of otherworldliness. And with reason, for there was much of it about him.

Valentino was born Rodolph Gugueleimi in the village of Castellaneta in southern Italy of a French mother and an Italian father. When eighteen he went to Paris and a year later migrated to New York City. It is known that he worked as a landscape gardener, a dishwasher, and a paid dancing partner, or gigolo. After a couple of years he secured occasional vaudeville work as a partner of female dancers of more reputation than his own.

Improvident by nature, with expensive tastes, Valentino lived from day to day as best he could. All his life he was in debt, from $1 to $100,000, according to his status. Being fully convinced that a supernatural "power" watched over him, he did not worry.

Mortal men found this power of Valentino's hard to deal with. We raised his salary far above the terms of his contract. That seemingly only whetted the power's appetite. It became downright unreasonable after *Blood and Sand,* with the lads of America imitating Valentino and women organizing worshipful cults.

Evidently the power had mistakenly got the notion that we had agreed to make *Blood and Sand* in Spain. At any rate, the idea crept into Valentino's head. He became dissatisfied with his dressing quarters, wishing to be surrounded, apparently, in the splendor of a powerful sheik of the desert.

Valentino rarely smiled on the screen or off, and I cannot recall ever having seen him laugh. It is true that he could be charming when he wished. In dealing with a lady interviewer, for example, he would give her a sort of look as if aware of something quite special in her, and treat her in an aloof but nevertheless cordial manner. On the other hand, he could be extremely temperamental.

Harry Reichenbach, the public relations genius who had reversed Sam Goldwyn's buzzer system, was now working for us. One day he called at Valentino's dressing room to discuss publicity matters.

"Does he know you?" a valet inquired.

"Well," Reichenbach replied, "he used to borrow two or three dollars at a time from me and always knew to whom to bring it back."

The valet went away but soon returned with word that his master was "resting."

It was my custom, as it had been in the old Twenty-sixth Street studio, to go out on the sets every morning when in Hollywood. This provided an opportunity to get better acquainted with the players and technicians. Besides putting me closer to production, I hoped that such visits would make everybody feel that the business office was more than a place where we made contracts and counted the money. The fact was that we kept as close tabs on the human element as on box-office receipts. Also,

I was secretly envious of those who had an intimate hand in production, and, making myself inconspicuous, often watched activities.

One day I was privileged to see a Valentino exhibition such as I had been hearing about. He was arguing with an assistant director—what about I did not know, and did not inquire. His face grew pale with fury, his eyes protruded in a wilder stare than any he had managed on the screen, and his whole body commenced to quiver. He was obviously in, or near, a state of hysteria. I departed as quietly as I had come.

The situation grew worse instead of better, and finally Valentino departed from the studios, making it plain that he had no intention of returning. We secured an injunction preventing him from appearing on the screen for anybody else. This did not bother him very much. He went on a lucrative dancing tour and was able to borrow all the money he needed.

Valentino was married but the relationship had not lasted long although it was still in technical force. Now he was in love with a beautiful girl named Winifred O'Shaughnessy. Her mother had married Richard Hudnut, cosmetics manufacturer, and Winifred sometimes used his surname. She preferred, however, to be known as Natacha Rambova, a name of her own choosing. She was art director for Alla Nazimova, the celebrated Russian actress who was one of our stars. Like Valentino, Natacha believed herself to be guided by a supernatural power.

They were married before Valentino's divorce decree

was final, and he was arrested in Los Angeles for bigamy. He got out of that by convincing authorities that the marriage had never been consummated, and the ceremony was repeated as soon as legal obstacles were cleared away.

Natacha Rambova appeared, as Valentino's business agent wrote later, "cold, mysterious, Oriental." She affected Oriental garb and manners. Yet she had served Alla Nazimova competently, was familiar with picture-making, and we felt she would be a good influence on Valentino. At any rate she brought him back to us.

Now, as it turned out, we had two Powers to deal with. She was the stronger personality of the two, or else her power secured domination over his. It was our custom to give stars a good deal of contractual leeway in their material. Natacha began to insert herself into the smallest details and he backed her in everything. His new pictures, *Monsieur Beaucaire* and *The Sainted Devil,* were less successful than those which had gone before.

The Valentino cults continued to blossom, but his publicity was not always good. Newspapers poked fun at the sleek hair and powdered faces of the "sheiks." The situation was not helped when it became known that Valentino wore a slave bracelet. Many people believed it to be a publicity stunt. But the fact was that Natacha Rambova had given it to him. Any suggestion that he discard it sent him into a rage.

A book he published, titled *Day Dreams,* caused raised eyebrows. Both he and his Natacha believed in automatic writing and it seems that the real author was his power, or the combined powers, working through him. An item titled "Your Kiss" is a good sample.

Your kiss,
A flame
  Of Passion's fire,
The sensitive Seal
  Of Love
In the desire,
  The fragrance
    Of your Caress;
Alas
  At times
    I find
      Exquisite bitterness
In
Your kiss.

We did not care to renew Valentino's contract, particularly since he and his wife wanted even more control over his pictures. He made arrangements with a new company, founded for the purpose, and work was begun on a film titled variously *The Scarlet Power* and *The Hooded Falcon,* dealing with the Moors in early Spain. Author of the story was Natacha Rambova.

After the two had spent eighty thousand dollars traveling in Europe for background material and exotic props, the story was put aside. Another, *Cobra,* was substituted with Natacha in full charge. It did poorly and the venture with the new company was at an end.

Joseph Schenck was now handling the business affairs

of United Artists, and he took a chance with Valentino—being careful to draw the papers in a manner keeping decisions out of the hands of either Valentino or Natacha. Valentino accepted the terms, though reluctantly. Not long afterward the couple separated and Natacha sued for divorce.

United Artists filmed *The Son of the Sheik,* which, as it turned out, was the celebrated lover's final picture.

Valentino's publicity became increasingly less favorable. He called his Hollywood home The Falcon's Lair, which opened him to some ridicule. The fun poked at the "sheiks" increased as the title of his new picture became known. Valentino himself grew more irritable.

He was in Chicago when the Chicago *Tribune* carried an editorial headed "The Pink Powder Puffs." One of the editorial writers, it seems, had visited the men's rest room of a popular dance emporium and there noted a coin device containing face powder. Many of the young men carried their own powder puffs, and they could hold it under the machine and by inserting a coin get a sprinkle of powder. The editorial, taking this situation as its theme, viewed the younger male generation with alarm. Most of the blame was placed on "Rudy, the beautiful gardener's boy," and sorrow was expressed that he had not been drowned long ago. In an earlier editorial the *Tribune* had made fun of his slave bracelet.

Valentino's "face paled, his eyes blazed, and his muscles stiffened" when he saw it—according to the later account of his business manager. Seizing a pen, Valentino addressed an open letter "To the Man (?) Who

Wrote the Editorial Headed 'The Pink Powder Puffs.' " He handed it to a rival newspaper.

"I call you a contemptible coward," Valentino had flung at the editorial writer, inviting him to come out from behind his anonymity for either a boxing or wrestling contest. After expressing hope that "I will have an opportunity to demonstrate to you that the wrist under the slave bracelet may snap a real fist into your sagging jaw," he closed with "Utter Contempt."

That was in August, 1925. Valentino came on to New York, and I was surprised to receive a telephone call from him inviting me to lunch.

"It is only that I would like to see you," Valentino said. "No business."

I would have agreed in any circumstance, but I was sure that he was telling the truth about not coming with a business proposition, since he was well set with United Artists.

"Certainly," I answered. "Where?"

"The Colony."

I had already guessed his choice, since The Colony was probably New York's most expensive restaurant. He liked the best. We set the time.

Valentino and I had barely reached The Colony when it became apparent that every woman in the place having the slightest acquaintance with me felt an irresistible urge to rush to my table with greetings. Though overwhelmed, I remained in sufficient command of my senses to observe the amenities by introducing each to Valentino.

He was thirty-one at this time, apparently in the best of physical condition, and, in this atmosphere at least, was relaxed. I do not know whether his divorce decree was yet final, but Natacha Rambova was in Paris. Recently Valentino's name had been linked with that of Pola Negri, one of our major stars.

"I only wanted to tell you," Valentino said after things had quieted down, "that I'm sorry about the trouble I made—my strike against the studio and all that. I was wrong and now I want to get it off my conscience by saying so."

I shrugged. "It's water over the dam. In this business if we can't disagree, sometimes violently, and then forget about it we'll never get anywhere. You're young. Many good years are ahead of you."

And so we dropped that line of talk. Valentino truly loved artistic things. He spoke of his ambition, when the time of his romantic roles was over, to direct pictures. I had the feeling that here was a young man to whom fame—and of a rather odd sort—had come too rapidly upon the heels of lean years, and he hadn't known the best way to deal with it.

"Telephone me any time," I said as we parted, "and we'll do this again. I enjoyed myself." And I had.

A day or two later I picked up a newspaper with headlines that Valentino had been stricken with appendicitis. At first it was believed that he was in no danger. But he took a turn for the worse. Joseph Schenck and his wife Norma Talmadge came to our home to wait out the crisis. Schenck was bringing encouraging reports from the hospital, when suddenly there was a relapse.

Valentino died half an hour past noon on August 23, 1925. It was a week to the minute since our meeting for lunch.

I, for one, was stunned by the hysteria which followed Valentino's death. In London a female dancer committed suicide. In New York a woman shot herself on a heap of Valentino's photographs.

A call came through to me from Hollywood. "Pola Negri is overwrought, and she's heading to New York for the funeral."

"Put a nurse and a publicity man on the train," I said, "and ask Pola to guard her statements to the press."

After Pola's arrival, my wife and I called at her hotel to offer condolences. Though very much upset, she intended to remain in seclusion as much as possible.

Valentino's body was laid in state at Campbell's Funeral Home at Broadway and Sixty-sixth Street, with the announcement that the public would be allowed to view it. Immediately a crowd of thirty thousand, mostly women, gathered.

Rioting—described as the worst in the city's history—began as police tried to form orderly lines. Windows were smashed. A dozen mounted policemen charged into the crowd time and time again. After one retreat of the crowd, twenty-eight women's shoes were gathered up. Women then rubbed soap on the pavement to make the horses slip.

The funeral home was now barred to the public—

those who got in had nearly wrecked the place by snatching souvenirs—but next day another crowd gathered when news spread that Pola Negri was coming to mourn. She was spirited in through a side door. Word soon came out that she had collapsed at the bier, which she had, and for some reason it excited the crowd.

On the day of the funeral 100,000 persons, again mainly women, lined the street in the neighborhood of the church in which it was being held. I was an honorary pallbearer, along with Marcus Loew, Joseph Schenck, Douglas Fairbanks, and others from the industry. Natacha Rambova was not present, being still abroad. But Valentino's first wife, actress Jean Acker, collapsed, and Pola Negri, heavily veiled, was for many moments on the point of swooning once more.

As the funeral procession left the church, the throngs fell silent except for subdued weeping of many of the women. The body was sent to Los Angeles for burial. The Valentino cult, I am told, is still in existence. At any rate, enough women visit his grave every year to have provided the gravekeeper with enough material for a book about them.

18

GLORIA SWANSON had become the "Queen of the Movies," or so the fan magazines called her, as the sweet ingénue made way for the glamor girl. Queen Gloria's throne was contested by exotic Pola Negri—especially on our own lot. We had to walk the line between the two very carefully. If one was given a service or a favor that was denied the other, the studio would in all likelihood have been shaken to the ground. Then along came Clara Bow, the "It" girl, symbol of the jazz age, and inhibitions flew to the winds.

While glamor reigned in the twenties, it by no means drove everything else off the screen. Two of our greatest successes were *The Covered Wagon* and *The Ten Commandments.*

I always mention *The Covered Wagon* as an illustration of one of the most important factors in picturemaking. In nearly every popular film there is a sequence, lasting perhaps no more than a moment or two, which swings the tide of audience approval. Again, some incident will tie a picture together or lift it in such a way that audiences go away feeling they have seen a great picture. Except for those few scenes patrons would have been vaguely dissatisfied without knowing exactly why.

Based on Emerson Hough's novel of the same name, *The Covered Wagon* was, as might be supposed, a story of a wagon train of pioneers crossing the plains and mountains. The period was the late 1840's and the settlers, headed for Oregon, faced incredible hardships. Wagons broke down, Indians attacked, the mountains exhausted humans and beasts alike. A part of the train deserted when news of the California gold rush came.

The picture was brilliantly directed by James Cruze. The romantic leads were J. Warren Kerrigan and Lois Wilson, but love interest was not a major element. Ernest Torrence as the guide and Tully Marshall as an old plains trader carried off a major share of the acting honors.

After the film was completed, Jesse Lasky and I viewed it together in a projection room.

"Jesse," I said as the lights went up, "do you remember, as the cost of this picture rose and rose, I telephoned you in Hollywood and asked what was going on?"

He laughed. "Naturally. And I replied that it was an epic. Such being the case, you said, you'd figure out a way to increase the budget."

I nodded. "It looks like an epic. It costs like an epic. But I do not feel it."

Lasky's response to the film was similar to my own. "I've been mulling over an idea," he said. "See how it strikes you. When the wagon train reaches Oregon, a settler might turn over a shovelful of dirt. It would be rich, black loam, a symbol of victory after the hardships. They are God-fearing people and the natural thing in a situation like that would be for them to fall on their knees and pray."

I was enthusiastic. "You make that sequence and in the meantime we'll run some audience tests. Then we'll try with the new shots and see what happens."

As we had feared, the original version, while pleasing the audiences, did not send them out of the theater with quite the feeling we had hoped for. And in spite of all the advertising and ballyhoo which can be mustered, the early audience members must report favorably to their friends, and at once, if the picture is to be a smash hit.

The new sequence made all the difference in the world. It was a fine picture anyway and would have done well. But in my opinion Lasky's improvement lifted it into a class which has seldom been attained.

The Covered Wagon was released in 1923. Cecil De Mille followed it a year later with *The Ten Commandments,* one of his greatest epics (which he is now remaking on a grander scale than was possible in that day).

De Mille had long since gained star billing in his own right. Many theater managers put his name on the marquee above those of the stars. A story of the period which Cecil tells as a joke on me illustrates his value to our company.

In the late teens and twenties De Mille was a demon flyer. It was not enough that he piloted his own plane—

when aloft he dipped and turned and altogether took what seemed to me the wildest chances. Occasionally he would fly down low merely, he claimed, to see my sad face gazing up at him. I stood motionless, he said, as when he had seen me watching the fire at the Twenty-sixth Street studio.

I don't know how I looked or how I stood. But certainly I spent a good deal of time pleading with him not to fly, or, if he did, to take fewer risks. He paid no heed so far as I could tell.

Cecil was, and is, a man of terrific energy—as his forty years of film producing show. He even found time to be a director of two or three or perhaps more banks. This served as a basis for another of his jokes. One of his pictures had not come up in my opinion to his standard.

"The trouble with you, Cecil," he quotes me as saying, "is that you are too many bankers."

I would not argue with him on a quotation because he has a fabulous memory and a remarkable command of details. He makes copious notes and files everything. In his work nothing is left to chance. When planning his Academy-Award-winning *The Greatest Show on Earth,* for example, he was hauled in a rigger's chair to the top of the Ringling Bros.-Barnum & Bailey big tent time and time again to study angles for trapeze scenes. It was hot up there and on inquiry he found that trapeze artists often are bothered by sweating palms. He suggested that air vents be made at the top, guarded against the rain by a canvas roof a few inches above the main one.

When the tent was redesigned his suggestion was carried into effect.

But to get back to the glamorous twenties. After De Mille had launched Gloria Swanson as a major star in *Male and Female*, he had used her as a sophisticated clotheshorse, mostly in drawing-room stories. Gloria's heyday was in the early and middle twenties when, under various directors, she starred in, among others, *The Gilded Cage, Prodigal Daughters, A Society Scandal, Manhandled, Wages of Virtue,* and *The Humming Bird.*

Born in Chicago in 1899, daughter of an Army captain, Gloria was a reigning queen while still in her early twenties. As a young girl she had been a notions-counter clerk, had played bit roles in the Essanay studio in Chicago and, as noted earlier, was in Hollywood and playing in Mack Sennett comedies when she was sixteen. A year later she married a rising young "heavy" named Wallace Beery.

Gloria was a trim girl of 5′1″ when she became a star. Curiously, she grew an inch during her twenties. She was no great beauty, but her face, with big silver-blue eyes and wide mouth with even teeth, photographed well. After graduating from her glamorous clotheshorse roles she developed into a competent actress.

Queen Gloria was a fabulous star in that fabulous period which social historians like to call the Era of Wonderful Nonsense. By now the lid was pretty well battened down on Hollywood and the water reduced to several degrees under boiling. But the public wanted glamor and Gloria was happy to fill the need. The magazines were filled with stories of her gold bathtub, slinky clothes, and the general atmosphere of luxury in which she dwelt.

On the set Queen Gloria could be temperamental, refusing to make scenes over, criticizing her wardrobe, the scenery, or her dressing quarters. But finally someone would say, "Look, Gloria, we've got to get the work done," and she would come down to earth. The little Chicago west side girl was never far below the glamorous surface.

The background of Pola Negri was genuinely exotic. She was born Appolonia Chalupec in Yanova, Russian Poland, in 1897. Her father, fiery and daring, was of gypsy blood—yet a revolutionary Polish patriot battling the czar for Polish independence. As a result he was exiled to Siberia, where he died. Cossacks burned the roof over the heads of Appolonia and her mother. In time the little girl was placed in the Imperial Ballet school in St. Petersburg. But instead of becoming a ballet dancer she eventually went on the Warsaw stage in dramatic roles.

Being fond of the works of Ada Negri, Italian poetess, Appolonia adopted Negri as her stage name and reduced her first name to Pola. At twenty she was in Berlin with Max Reinhardt, the celebrated stage producer, and soon was the toast of the German capital. In the meantime she had married Count Eugene Dombski and thus, although the marriage had not lasted, was an authentic countess.

After seeing Negri in Ernst Lubitsch's *Gypsy Blood,* we sought to bring her to America. Other companies had the same idea. Al Kaufman, after serving in the armed forces, had remained in Europe, and to him was assigned the task of getting her name on a contract. The postwar inflation in Germany was in full swing and Al's arms ached from carrying bales of marks about before his goal was accomplished.

The impact on America of the Countess Negri was sensational. Writers described her as an "exquisite woman of the world," and were struck by her fluency in Italian, French, German, Russian, and Polish—also with her bright eyes and jet-black hair and the striking shifts of her moods.

Hollywood society did not take kindly, however, to the scintillating star from abroad. She intimated that, culturally speaking, the community was some distance below her standards, and she withdrew, as she said, to her music and books to escape the boring parties. I do not know whether she openly snubbed Queen Gloria—and certainly she did not if we were able to prevent it—but the rivalry was soon hot. Maybe each had spies in the palace of the other. At any rate, we could depend on it that a penny spent for one would be followed by the demand of a penny for the other.

The Swanson-Negri situation was partly responsible for our willingness to allow Gloria to make *Madame Sans Gene,* one of her major vehicles, in France. It was a story of a girl friend of young Napoleon's who later climbed to power amidst glamor and comedy. Pola wanted the role, but Gloria won the competition.

It was one thing for Queen Gloria to go to Paris, another for her to choose her own time. We wanted her to stay and make a picture here before commencing *Madame Sans Gene.* I was called upon to relay this information to her.

"It will take perhaps three months," I said. "Then you will be perfectly free to go."

Queen Gloria answered, "I am going now."

We gathered our forces into council and solemnly vowed to put our foot down. The task once more fell to me.

"Gloria," I said sternly, "we have thought the matter over very carefully and concluded that you must remain here for the three-month period which I mentioned before."

This statement I followed with some thousands of words of what I regarded as clinching arguments.

Gloria did not say anything.

A couple of weeks later I ran into her in a Paris bar.

"Join us," she said, as if nothing had happened.

After the introductions I sat down at her table as if nothing had happened.

To help with the French language, our Paris studio had assigned an affable, good-looking young male employee to Gloria. Around the studio he was called Hank. Outside, he was more formally—and properly—known as the Marquis de la Falaise de la Coudray.

He was in the party and it soon became apparent that

Gloria was in much need of help with her French. She had divorced Wallace Beery and since then had married and divorced a businessman named Somborn, founder of Hollywood's Brown Derby restaurant.

Gloria and the marquis were married after the completion of *Madame Sans Gene*. It was a grand ceremony and at the end, like everybody else, I went up to wish them well.

She drew me a little aside. "I see that you've just thrown a big party for Pola Negri at the Ritz in New York."

I nodded.

"It would be nice if you were to have a party at the Ritz for us when we arrive."

I nodded.

After the Ritz party, Gloria wanted to hurry with her consort to Hollywood. The only space we could find available was on a train loaded with our own people, mostly salesmen, on the way to a convention. Gloria was royalty at the start, which was understandable now that a new title was piled on top of the old. But she thawed rapidly. Before long she was a big participator in crap games.

The affable marquis was soon called Hank by everyone on the train, as he had been in the Paris studio. There were, however, a number of blank spots in his knowledge of America. Though not believing that the West was as wild as formerly, he was sure that Indians still occasionally went on the warpath and that six-gun toters were not yet fully under control.

Naturally he was reassured. Gloria herself told him that trains were not attacked by Indians very often and a holdup was nowadays a rarity.

There was to be a stop of a few hours in Albuquerque, New Mexico, and several of our people offered to take Hank on a tour of the town and countryside. They would wire ahead, they said, to insure that plenty of peace officers were on hand for protection. They did wire ahead.

The automobiles carrying Hank and his new friends—as well as some purported scouts and experienced gun-fighters—was attacked by Indians about a mile outside Albuquerque. The redskins were at last driven off, but not before Hank's opinion of the Wild West had been thoroughly confirmed in his mind.

Gloria had been away from Hollywood for a couple of years, having made a picture or two in New York before going to Paris. For her arrival the town outdid itself. A brass band met her at the station. Flowers—tons of them—were strewn in the streets. At the showing of *Madame Sans Gene* the audience rose and sang *Home Sweet Home.*

After that Gloria and I took up the matter of renewing her contract. My offer was eighteen thousand dollars a week, and I was prepared to go somewhat higher, perhaps to a flat million dollars a year. Gloria said no, she wanted to make pictures of a more artistic nature and therefore wished to produce on her own after working out her contract.

She did, and with a good deal of success in the beginning, especially with *Sadie Thompson,* a version of Somerset Maugham's *Rain.* But the reign of Queen Gloria was over. A few years ago she played for us once more in *Sunset Boulevard* in the role of a star of the past. In the picture the former star one night ran some of her old films. A few of the scenes of the picture-within-a-picture were taken from *Queen Kelly,* an expensive film produced by Gloria but never released.

19

IN this chapter I will turn from pictures and players to report on a few other things which have interested me along the way.

One item concerns a scenario writer—fellow by the name of Franklin D. Roosevelt. He submitted only one, true enough. But it was a whopper and the trouble it caused us equaled that of a dozen run-of-the-mill scripts. The fault, I hasten to add, was all our own.

During the First World War my son Eugene had wanted—though under age—to join the Navy, and I had given the parental consent required. After the initial training he was assigned to the Bureau of Ordnance and stationed in Washington. One of his duties was to carry top-secret messages to the young Assistant Secretary of the Navy, Franklin Roosevelt.

It seemed to Eugene that, while the sheafs he delivered were important, Roosevelt was on the whole rather lonely. At any rate, he often asked Eugene, an enlisted man, to sit down for a talk. After Roosevelt connected the name Zukor with Famous Players-Lasky there was a good deal of discussion of films and film-making.

Roosevelt's civilian assistant and confidant, Louis Howe, was less cordial to Eugene. Everybody who has read Mrs. Roosevelt's books knows that Howe's great devotion to her husband made him jealous of others who entered the intimate circle even briefly. Howe was a gnomelike man who doubtless appeared sourer than he really was. To Eugene he would say, "Why didn't they send a man instead of a boy?" and things of a similar nature. Eugene stood in considerable awe of him.

A year or two after running unsuccessfully for the vice-presidency in 1920, Roosevelt was stricken with infantile paralysis. To occupy himself during his fight for recovery, he studied history, especially naval history. His particular hero was John Paul Jones, the American Revolutionary commander who, when little more than thirty, outfought the British on the high seas.

Roosevelt prepared a scenario of Jones' life and sent it—on April 24, 1923, according to the records—to us. The name Famous Players-Lasky had stuck in his memory from the conversations with Eugene.

The manuscript was a formidable document, measuring two to three inches thick. Eugene, back at the company, read it through. The form was not suitable for screening, but he sent it on to Hollywood for evaluation as a story.

To this day I do not understand how the people in the scenario department managed to lose such a bale of manuscript. But they accomplished it. Roosevelt's impact on the electorate during his campaign for the vice-presidency had not been great, and doubtless the scenario had been tossed in with those of other unknowns.

One day Eugene received a visit from Louis Howe, who had continued as Roosevelt's adviser. Eugene, unhappy over loss of the manuscript, and doubtless affected by Howe's former critical attitude, began to turn over both east and west coast offices frantically. Howe sensed that something was wrong and he kept in hot pursuit with telephone calls and personal appearances.

I was very upset. A note came from Roosevelt: "I have need of this manuscript immediately." I could reply only that we were deeply ashamed, that I had taken steps to tighten up the story department—but still we had not been able to find his scenario. We never did.

Eugene joined the Navy again during World War II. One of his early assignments was to attend White House press conferences. On his first visit the room was crowded and he could not find a chair or hardly a place from which to see and hear. He was dodging and ducking about, trying to find a peephole, when a voice called, "Zukor, get a chair and bring it in here."

The voice was the President's, and of course a space was cleared. When the conference was over, Eugene was asked to remain.

"Where," the President demanded accusingly, "is my scenario?" Then he threw back his head and laughed.

Eugene was able to laugh, too, since he knew that

Roosevelt had been able to prepare a suitable copy from old drafts. They had a pleasant chat, remembering the old days in the Navy Department.

Roosevelt was an excellent historian, but nations differ widely in their views of what happened, and I am afraid that had his scenario been of a professional caliber, and had we screened it, a terrible storm would have arisen in England. Roosevelt had been something less than magnanimous in his treatment of the foes of his hero John Paul Jones.

What small excuse existed for losing a manuscript lay in the rapid growth of the movie industry, and our organization with it, which prevented us from ever tying things up in neat packages. Even the short depression of the early twenties affected the industry very little. It has long since been demonstrated, of course, that the economy of the later twenties was not so healthy as had been supposed. Yet most business was booming and the movie industry, coming from practically nothing to be the fifth largest of the land, was skyrocketing faster than any.

After turning the corner of fifty, in 1923, I was finding —or anyhow taking—more time for relaxation. A few years earlier I had purchased a thousand-acre tract in Rockland County, up the Hudson River from New York City. It lay near the village of New City. I was developing it slowly, enjoying every minute. Because I always referred to it as my "farm," and thought of it that way, my friends had an excuse for kidding me. The average farm, they liked to point out, did not have an eighteen-hole golf course, a swimming pool, or even a filling station where guests might tank-up free.

My chief pleasures, nevertheless, were in planting trees, laying out gardens, and planning such structures as we needed. There were animals, too—especially cows. We had an up-to-date dairy which produced an excellent quality and quantity of milk. As it happened, there was an orphanage nearby and we gave most of our milk to it.

I will not contend that existence at Mountainview Farm, as we called it, was an example of the simple life. Yet the scale was far from magnificent. For building material we used Rockland County field stone.

The "day house" was something like a mountain lodge. There were animal heads on the walls, rugs scattered about, and altogether the atmosphere was a relaxed one. The main kitchen was in the day house and the larger dinners were served here.

There was a guest house which we endeavored to keep filled over the week ends, and did. My wife and I liked to keep the place filled with relatives and friends, including many of the stars. An interviewer once said I was a good host because I comprised a fine one-man audience.

After the children were married, we built the "children's house." It contained a suite for each of the two families and another for guests with children. The more children running about the place, the more we liked it.

The clubhouse was for golfers and swimmers and other sports enthusiasts. My favorite game—aside from cards—was golf. The clubhouse also had a small movie theater in it.

In the old days in the fur business, Marcus Loew's and my families had lived cater-cornered from one another on Seventh Avenue in New York City. Now we were neighbors again, the Loews occupying a Georgian mansion which a silver king had thrown up.

Loew had come into movie production, buying first into Metro, and extending it into Metro-Goldwyn-Mayer. This was pleasant because we could sit on the veranda and make fun of each other's pictures. Our company had starred Enrico Caruso in a film titled *My Cousin.* The great opera star's voice naturally could not be used and Marcus claimed the picture was the greatest bust in all history. I was never able to argue him down on that point, and never tried to very hard.

One of the high points in the twenties for me was the dedication, in 1926, of the Paramount Building, occupying the Broadway block between Forty-third and Forty-fourth streets in Times Square—including the site of the old Shanley Restaurant. The building is thirty-three stories high and contains the vast Paramount Theatre.

Thomas A. Edison, as I said earlier, was there, along with many other notables. To me it was not simply a mark of success of the movie industry or of myself in it. It was a symbol of the opportunities in America, and my mind was less on that great structure of stone and steel, which cost seventeen million dollars, than on my life in Hungary and the journey to the United States with a few dollars sewn into my vest.

Construction of the Paramount Theatre was in a way the capstone of my policy of "showplaces" for films, launched first with my successful effort to get Mitchell Mark to devote his Strand Theatre exclusively to pictures. Our company had used the Strand for New York openings until Mark entered the First National group. As a result of that we had purchased the spacious Rivoli and Rialto theaters in the Times Square district.

By now there were first-run houses, many of them owned by us, in all the major cities and the "movie palace" idea was catching on in the smaller ones also. A picture which got a good send-off in a "palace," especially one of Broadway's, was almost certain to do well everywhere.

An important leader in the movie-theater field was the firm of Balaban & Katz, which owned the great Chicago houses. The Balaban part had been launched by Barney and A. J. Balaban, sons of a fish-store owner, while they were still in their teens. The Katz part was Sam Katz, who as a young boy had played the piano in Carl Laemmle's first store theater in Chicago. Sam had been a millionaire theater magnate while still in college.

In 1917 the Balabans, now including several younger brothers, had combined with the Katz forces. Sam's father had closed his barber shop to go into business with him. Now Sam Katz, still in his early thirties, had taken leave from Balaban & Katz to head Publix Theaters, a subsidiary of Famous Players-Lasky.

We had various other subsidiaries or were financially interested in other companies from time to time. But to follow their structure would only mean inclusion of a mass of dry details.

In running through an old *Photoplay* magazine, I noticed an item describing charges that "Adolph Zukor's company has a sinister design to gobble the industry." That was rather typical. If I wasn't gobbling the industry, I was swallowing it. For dinner, it seemed, I started off with a theater or two, followed with a producing company, and ended with a few stars lured from other companies, served up with cream and sugar. This was mildly amusing in view of the fact that the motion picture industry was, and is, the most competitive of any I have ever heard about.

When radio grew strong in the middle twenties, many believed that it would ruin the film business. I thought it would help by creating new talent. We brought radio people to the screen and put screen people on the air. To help boost radio, we secured a half interest in the Columbia Broadcasting System. Earlier, after Charles Frohman had lost his life in the sinking of the *Lusitania*, we had bought his theatrical producing company and had continued it. Partly to make better use of New York's stage talent, we had built a two million-dollar studio on nearby Long Island. Our aim was to keep the amusement industry as a whole on as high and broad a plane as possible.

The policy of film "showcases" was extended to Europe with the building of the Carleton and Plaza theaters in London, the Paramount in Paris, and others in Vienna and elsewhere. We were making numerous pictures abroad too. Therefore I traveled a good deal. It was always a pleasure to visit my older brother Arthur, who had become a distinguished rabbi in Berlin. Sometimes I returned to Ricse. It was satisfying to have my parents' old store and home reconstructed, the church and school renovated, and a town well drilled.

Some people, however, overestimated the wealth of the Americans. One day I visited the grave of my parents and such a crowd of mourners I never saw. From far and wide people had arrived for the purpose of adopting me as a relative.

In the spring of 1927, I was traveling in Europe but paying close attention to the papers for news of the trans-Atlantic flyers who were poised to take off from America. I was particularly interested in Commander Richard E. Byrd because I had participated in the financing of his North Pole expedition a year or two earlier and had met him on several occasions. Byrd and his pilot, Bert Acosta, a Frenchman, were awaiting what they considered favorable weather. So was Clarence Chamberlin and his crew.

In Paris, Al Kaufman and I were catching a train to Amsterdam when we heard a newsboy shouting something about a trans-Atlantic plane. While Al ran to buy a paper I boarded the train confident that Byrd and Acosta were in flight.

Al came in shaking his head in wonderment. "Some fellow took off alone in a small plane," Al said. "He must be crazy."

"Well," I said, "he may have started, but surely he has turned back by this time."

Al sat down. "Might be. The fellow's name is Lindbergh, 'Slim' Lindbergh, they call him, and he was a mail pilot out around St. Louis. He calls his plane *The Spirit of St. Louis.*"

Our compartment was shared by a Frenchman who listened politely. As soon as Al was finished with the paper he asked if he might see it. He clucked sadly as he read.

I said reassuringly, "Oh, he has certainly turned back."

"No," the Frenchman said, "I do not believe he has. My profession is aeronautics and my office has been alive with reports and conjectures ever since this young man began his flight. He has been sighted at sea, and he was a long way from home."

Naturally our interest was aroused by the opinions of an expert. We asked for the percentages on success.

"Not a chance, not a chance," the Frenchman answered, shaking his head regretfully. "Imagine! This man would have to stay awake for thirty or forty or even fifty hours, a difficult feat in itself. All this time he must be alert. And what about storms and even ordinary mechanical difficulties? No, no. Impossible."

In Amsterdam we followed the sketchy bulletins of Lindbergh's flight. All Europe, like America, was becoming excited as the lone flyer rode on. When returning to Paris we found the same aeronautics expert aboard the train. Of course we joined him and two or three other experts happened to be with him.

"It is remarkable so far," the Frenchman said. "But even if this man should arrive over Le Bourget Field, he can never land safely. He will be too tired, his reflexes will be off. No man who has been in the air more than a 24-hour day can land a plane safely."

The other experts agreed. They were rooting for the young flyer, but they were certain of his doom.

Paris was boiling with excitement. In the evening Al and I, in company with what seemed the whole of the city, went to Le Bourget Field. Excitement grew as word spread that the flyer had been positively identified over Ireland, winging on the last lap of his sensational journey.

A great cry went up as a small plane came into the range of the searchlights and headed for a landing. I watched with bated breath for the wheels to touch, remembering the words of the experts. The tires made contact, and my heart leapt into my throat as the plane bounced crazily. But it righted itself as the crowd burst through the police cordons.

It was a mail plane making its usual run.

"If that pilot had so much trouble," I said to Al, "how in the world can Lindbergh make it? Maybe we had better go." I had no desire to be a spectator at a man's death.

"No," Al said. "He's got that millionth chance. Let's stay here and pull for him."

After a while another plane was picked out by the searchlights. It glided down and landed soft as a feather.

It was Lindbergh.

In his pocket were letters of introduction to Ambassador Herrick, which he hoped would get him a bath and a change of clothing. The crowd naturally tossed the young flyer on its shoulders and carried him from his plane in triumph.

Next day Al and I were guests of Ambassador Herrick at a luncheon for Lindbergh, at which he delivered his famous "We" speech—referring to his plane and himself. After it was over, Al went outside and bought two pictures of the new hero from a vendor.

During the informal period after the luncheon Al took the pictures to Lindbergh and asked him to sign them. The slim flyer looked surprised. It evidently had not occurred to him that anybody might want his picture, or especially would take the trouble to ask him to sign it. Then, smiling, he took Al's pen.

"Make one to Adolph Zukor," Al said. He spelled the name and then gave his own.

So it is possible that I have Lindbergh's first autograph. I am not a collector, but I keep the signed picture along with one of Queen Mary and myself, taken while she was visiting our English studios, which she inscribed to me. Whenever I pass the Paramount Theatre's stage door and see the notebook-armed kids awaiting some current favorite who is appearing in person, I have an inkling of what motivates them.

20

JUST as the land was overrun with the "sheiks" in Valentino's heyday, there came into being a million or so "It" girls after Clara Bow's 1927 picture entitled simply *It.* The result, it must be granted, was a kind of national consternation. Already the flappers had bobbed their hair and rolled their stockings. Now teen-age girls —and many a little older—displayed extraordinary brashness, making a point, usually a loud one, of caring not a tinker's dam what anybody thought about them.

"It" became synonymous with sex appeal—abbreviated in that day to "S.A."—but the definition by the originator of the term, Elinor Glyn, was more complicated. "It" was personal magnetism, a naturalness of manner, a lack of self-consciousness. A possessor of "It" was, in short, a true child of nature, uncaring of what other people thought. There were "It" boys, of course, but the term came to be applied mainly to girls.

Clara Bow had served, with reason, as Elinor Glyn's model for the "It" personality. Clara was exactly the same off the screen as on. She danced even when her feet were not moving. Some part of her was in motion in all her waking moments—if only her great rolling eyes. Though not beautiful, Clara was a striking girl, with red hair, a soft heart-shaped face, and a plump figure. Yet it was an elemental magnetism—sometimes described as animal vitality—that made her the center of attraction in any company.

Clara truly did not care what people thought about her—didn't notice. But her warm personality and spontaneous generosity made her popular with those about her. A few studio spats occurred, inevitably. Clara and Pola Negri were once assigned to adjoining sets. Clara was playing jazz tunes to get everybody in a proper frame of mind for a hot-cha scene. Pola was dying with the help of sad mood music.

The principals took a break from their dancing and dying long enough to engage in a number of high, hard words. In time their respective directors managed to work out a musical compromise.

A true product of the Jazz Age, Clara was typical of her generation even to the point of having applied for a motion picture job via the fan magazines. The chief difference was that she got it. The story runs that the photograph which opened the way was actually mailed to the magazine by her father, Robert Bow, a day laborer. The Bows lived in meager circumstances on Church Street in Brooklyn. Her mother opposed Clara's wish to enter pictures, but she died while Clara was in her early teens, and afterward Robert Bow pressed his daughter's chances as best he could.

Victory in the fan-magazine contest gained a small part for Clara in a film called *Down to the Sea in Ships,* made in an eastern studio. Though it led to nothing else immediately, Robert Bow succeeded in interesting an agent, Maxine Alton, in Clara's potentialities. The agent began to hunt roles for Clara and managed to get a part or two for her in shoestring ventures. Finally Ben Schulberg, who was producing independently, took an interest in the Brooklyn redhead, now in her late teens. After seeing her in bit parts he sent for her to come to Hollywood for a test.

Maxine Alton later described her cross-country train journey with the uninhibited "It" girl of the future. Clara arrived at Grand Central Station carrying a pathetic little satchel and a cheap portable phonograph. She had a single record—"Dance of the Wooden Soldiers." Once aboard the train, Clara unlimbered the machine and turned it on full blast. During the next few days it rarely stopped.

Clara's experience with trains had been limited to the subway. She wanted to know who was in charge of the train, and when told that it was the conductor, she began to worry about him. She asked how he managed to get any sleep.

"It's four days since we left New York," she said, "and he hasn't stopped the damn train long enough to get himself a plug of tobacco."

She was fascinated but confused upon hearing that flowers could be telegraphed.

"Suppose you do manage to get them over the wires," she said. "How'll you keep 'em fresh?"

Before the journey was over Clara's thick red hair stood on end, her cheap dresses were shapeless, and "Dance of the Wooden Soldiers" was full of spine-chilling shrieks. But Clara was a smash hit with all the passengers. Her magnetism was not to be denied.

Ben Schulberg was not so sure of the magnetism when he saw her, still bedraggled. But he directed her in a scene or two and found that she laughed or cried with equal ease, could turn her emotions on and off at will. Later Schulberg came back to our company—the reader will remember that he was Famous Players' first publicity man—as studio manager and brought Clara with him.

Clara was a star before *It*. But that picture marked an era, and I feel that the film's story is worthy of a rather full recollection here.

The picture begins in the office of a large department store where a tall, thin comic of the "pip, pip, old boy" school has opened *Cosmopolitan* magazine and is reading from Elinor Glyn's story "It" to the handsome young hero, who is taking over the store's management while his father, the owner, is away. The comic explains that with "It" men can win women, and vice versa. He brings out that the "It" person is without self-consciousness, caring nothing for the impression made on others.

The hero, paying little attention, starts out for an inspection of the store, followed by the comic, still holding the magazine and ostentatiously looking for somebody possessing "It." Eventually they arrive in the neighborhood of Clara, who works behind the lingerie counter. Her hair is piled fluffily high, with bangs, and the sides come part way down her cheeks like scythes, emphasizing the heartlike shape of her face. She constantly dances and jiggles while waiting on customers. There is seldom, if ever, a moment in the entire picture when she is in repose.

All the shopgirls are enchanted with the boss's son, and the air is filled with smart cracks typical of the era. "Look, there's Hot Socks," one says. Another murmurs, "Sweet Santa Claus." Miffed at one of the girls, Clara threatens to "take the snap out of your garters." The hero pays no attention to Clara but the comic quite naturally sees in her the "It" girl for whom he is searching.

Clara overhears a remark that the hero will be dining at the Ritz that night, and when the foppish comic offers to drive her home she accepts with the provision that they use her car, a two-decker bus. The flowerpot hats, short skirts, rolled stockings, and gaudy garters of the day are much in evidence. On the stoop of her slum tenement home in Gashouse Gables, she accepts the comic's offer for dinner, provided they go to the Ritz. Though nonplused, he agrees.

In the flat which she shares with a sick girl friend and the friend's baby, Clara bounces and jiggles about happily. The friend wields scissors and needle until Clara's shop dress is a low-cut evening gown. The handiwork is topped off with a bouquet of artificial flowers.

The Ritz headwaiter looks down his nose at Clara's getup, but when the comic asks for a corner table, Clara rejects it. "I do not crave this table. When I'm in the swim I want to be with the goldfish." All this brings haughty looks from the customers, especially from a snobbish blonde and her dowager mother who are at a table with the hero.

In walks Elinor Glyn herself, a large, middle-aged woman. The hero, bored anyhow, goes to her table and asks for an explanation of "It" and is impressed with her explanation that it is naturalness, indifference to the impression made on others, and so forth. Meanwhile Clara carries on happily, pulling a wishbone with the comic, crying out at the sight of good things to eat, and of course bouncing and jiggling. All the while she is oblivious to the horrified stares of customers of high degree.

At last the hero notices that here is a girl with "It." In the lobby after dinner Clara overhears him say that he is smitten with her. Introduced by the comic, she bets him that he will not recognize her when they meet again.

Next day a woman customer is making a fuss at the lingerie counter as he passes and he stops to help her. Clara quickly substitutes another salesgirl. But when he orders that the salesgirl responsible must be sent to his office, she goes. Though not really intending to win the bet through subterfuge, Clara is piqued when a phone call comes through from the blonde, the hero's fiancée. She demands payment and sets the stakes as a trip to the seashore—Coney Island. They spend a rollicking evening in the Fun House, slick barrels, and the like.

After driving Clara home in his Rolls-Royce roadster, the hero steals a kiss. She slaps him. "You're one of those Minute Men," she cries. "Try to kiss a girl the minute you're out with her." That makes him ashamed of himself.

Now the story moves along as a couple of welfare workers try to take the baby away from Clara's friend on the ground that she cannot support it. Having a job, Clara poses as the mother and a loud scene develops. A tall young reporter, hat pulled low on his forehead, his lean jaws working, looks piercingly into the room and alertly writes his notes. (Gary Cooper didn't get any billing for the bit part.)

The comic happens to be present and between his later report to the hero and the newspaper story the romance of the boss's son and the shopgirl is in a bad way. Soon afterward Clara is called to his office with others to receive a bonus check. First he tries to snub her but, after the others have gone, admits his love, offering diamonds and other worldly goods. She weeps, realizing, as she says, that he is proposing a "left-handed arrangement." There is nothing for her to do in the circumstances except throw up her job.

The comic arrives at Gashouse Gables to "forgive" Clara, but learns the truth, and in the conversation it comes out that the hero is setting off on a yachting trip. Clara decides to join the party, force the hero to propose, and then laugh in his face. The comic is required to take her aboard incognito.

It was the day of the ukulele. Clara plays it and sings, bouncing up and down at what would now seem an alarming rate. The hero proposes and she refuses and laughs, but soon afterward weeps in private. The comic now tells the hero the truth, whereupon he sets out to find Clara, relinquishing the wheel to the comic. The yacht promptly hits a barge, throwing Clara and the blonde into the water. Clara saves the blonde, slugging her in the jaw in the process, and turns her over to the hero as he swims madly to the rescue. Then, saying she is going home, Clara swims away blowing water into the air. When the comic arrives in a rowboat, the hero puts the blonde in his charge and goes after Clara. She climbs on the anchor and when he can not find her immediately she drops a shoe on his head. He climbs on the anchor and the final love scene is right there, with the fade-out kiss showing Clara playfully twisting his ear.

Not strictly realism, perhaps. Even the "It" girls of that day would doubtless now regard the story as corny. But no one can see the picture without being struck by the likable vitality and true comic spirit of Clara Bow.

It apppeared as two eras were drawing toward a close. One was the Jazz Age itself. The other was that of silent films.

After a couple of decades the idea has arisen that the "talkies" came all in a rush—that one month the screen was silent and the next it talked. Actually, the changeover was slow, requiring several years.

The talking picture was not, of course, a new thing.

Edison and others had synchronized phonographic devices with films as early as the 1890's. Eugene Augustin Lauste, a former employee of Edison's, in 1907 demonstrated a device in London which seemed to have possibilities. Not long afterward a machine called the Synchroscope was put on the market in the United States and gained considerable attention.

Edison made progress with his Cameraphone, sometimes called Kinetophone, between 1908 and 1913. D. W. Griffith showed a picture called *Dream Street* in 1921 which contained some dialogue. For it a device called Photokinema was employed. Another pioneer, Dr. Lee De Forest, is credited with having shown the first sound-on-film talking pictures, a series of vaudeville shorts, at the Rivoli Theatre in New York City in 1923.

The industry watched all these experiments with interest. But it was felt that none had been perfected sufficiently for wide public use. There were twenty thousand motion picture theaters in the United States in 1926. Therefore a device had to be of proved efficiency to justify the enormous cost of installing sound equipment.

During the middle twenties the electrical engineers made great strides in recording and reproducing sound. This was true particularly in the laboratories of the General Electric Company and of the Bell Laboratories, jointly owned by the American Telephone and Telegraph Company and the Western Electric Company. These efforts were eventually to revolutionize the phonograph as well as the motion picture.

Sam Warner is credited with launching the movement

which finally resulted in the wide adoption of sound on film. After a visit to the Bell Laboratories he convinced his brothers, Harry, Albert, and Jack, that the time was ripe for sound pictures. Warner Brothers was licensed to use the Bell system in April, 1926. The Warner picture *Don Juan,* with John Barrymore, was immediately synchronized with a musical accompaniment by the New York Philharmonic Orchestra and was premiered on the evening of August 6, 1926, at the Warner Theatre in New York City.

Warner Brothers followed with *The Jazz Singer,* starring Al Jolson, which opened on October 6, 1927. This is widely believed to have been the first all-talking picture. Actually, Jolson's singing was the main feature of it, though he spoke a word or two. The first all-talking picture, Warner's *Lights of New York,* opened at the Strand Theatre on July 6, 1928.

The premiere of *The Jazz Singer* has gone down, however, as the most important historical date of talking pictures. Unhappily, tragedy accompanied it. Sam Warner had died suddenly only a few days earlier.

Meanwhile other companies had entered the field. Paramount (we were now releasing our films under this name rather than Famous Players-Lasky) had secured the Photophone, developed by the General Electric Company and the Radio Corporation of America. We used it for our epic air picture *Wings* (in which Gary Cooper rose to prominence) made toward the end of 1927. Fox was making progress with Movietone. Other companies were licensed by one system or another and there was no doubt that talking pictures were the great thing of the future.

Yet we had an obligation to those twenty thousand theaters while they were making their change-over. By the fall of 1929—two years after *The Jazz Singer*—only about one-fourth of them had managed it. Therefore we continued to produce silent pictures. Often we made a silent film and later made it over into a "talkie."

The consternation among silent players with the advent of sound was naturally very great. But the stories of sudden wreckage of careers has been vastly exaggerated. This is shown by a glance at the list of our major players as the silent era closed.

Among them were William Powell, Richard Dix, Bebe Daniels, George Bancroft, Clara Bow, Clive Brook, Nancy Carroll, Gary Cooper, Jean Arthur, Fay Wray, Florence Vidor, Emil Jannings, Adolph Menjou, Evelyn Brent, and Paul Lukas.

There were tense moments, of course, while voice tests were being made.

Jean Arthur listened to her playback and cried in despair, "A foghorn!" It was that foghorn quality which made her a greater star than she might have become on the silent screen.

William Powell heard his voice and raced out the door, shouting over his shoulder that he planned to go into hiding. Powell had been on the stage but, like many others, was amazed to hear his own voice.

It is true that the microphone helped some voices and took away from others. But most of those with real ability and determination adjusted to the new medium. There are always stars on their way down, and it was easy to blame sound for those who happened to be slipping.

It is widely believed, for example, that Clara Bow was finished by the "talkies." Her voice was actually quite good and she made talking pictures. But the unrestrained vitality which had been her great asset now was a curious handicap. The technicians had not learned to use the microphones as skillfully as they do today, and the players had to manage to stay near one of them, which was likely as not concealed in a bouquet of flowers, without giving the impression that the voice was being aimed into it.

Clara was too restless. She would be all over the set, and then, realizing that the microphone was not picking up her voice, would sometimes stand and curse it. Besides, the day of the flapper was over. Clara might have made a new career as an emotional actress or a mature comedienne. But the row would have been a hard one and she chose instead to retire.

The one great tragedy of sound was John Gilbert, Metro-Goldwyn-Mayer's sensational romantic star. His voice was too high—not effeminate, but with a piping note which all the efforts of the voice instructors could not bring into line with his screen appearance. His failure upset him emotionally and doubtless had much to do with his early death.

It was sometimes said that Emil Jannings, a great star for us after we had brought him from Germany, was a casualty of talking pictures. But he had been on the stage and other foreign players mastered their accents. Greta

Garbo did for Metro-Goldwyn-Mayer. Two of our players, Marlene Dietrich and Maurice Chevalier, were immediate sensations in talking pictures.

Maurice Chevalier is one of the greatest showmen of his time—which has been quite a long one. When he began making musicals for us in 1930, he was turning forty and already had been on the stage for a quarter of a century. The son of a Paris laborer, he had grown up in an Apache neighborhood, ending his schooling at the age of twelve. He was an apprentice carpenter and after that an apprentice acrobat. He didn't like the first and hurt himself in the second.

Long years of semi-starvation in the music halls followed. As a soldier in World War I, Chevalier was wounded and captured by the Germans. It was while in a prison camp that he learned to speak English.

I had been acquainted with Chevalier for many years, having often met him abroad. In describing him as a great showman I refer to much more than his stage personality and technique. A player who maintains a long career must know his abilities in relation to his audience. Chevalier never forgot that his basic audience was in France. He would depart long enough for stage appearances in England, America, and elsewhere. But he always hurried home, never giving the French a chance to forget him.

It was the same when he came to America to work for us. His plan, as I recall, was to make three pictures a year, one in Hollywood, one in New York, and one in Paris. He refused to tie himself down anywhere. He thinks things through, which is the main reason he is practically indestructible. One of these days he will be over here again, and, though rising sixty, will capture the new movie audiences as he did the old.

It is hardly necessary to describe the Chevalier who was a sensation in the early days of sound pictures. His protruding underlip, his straw hat, his disarming manner and charming songs were indelibly fixed in the public mind. Off the stage he is quiet and serious, but nonetheless enjoyable company. One time I left him in charge of Mountainview Farm for a couple of months while my wife and I were abroad. Once in Paris Mrs. Zukor and I went to see him on the stage, and, spotting us, he stopped the show to greet us. Chevalier is a man I always make a point of looking up when in Paris, and he looks me up when in New York. It is a tie of men who have spent half a century in show business, in addition to a long personal friendship.

Marlene Dietrich is another indestructible because above all she is an individual. I met her for the first time in Berlin, after her hit as a music hall singer with Emil Jannings in *The Blue Angel,* made in the German language. She had been a night-club and musical stage entertainer. Of course I had seen *The Blue Angel* and was aware of her screen potentialities. Yet I was struck at once with her high intelligence, humor, and force of character.

We had been fearful that the German beauty, though her screen personality was admittedly mysterious and exotic, would be taken by the public as an imitator of

Garbo. It was soon plain to me that Marlene's force of character was too great for her to be taken as the imitator of anyone for long.

Nevertheless, Marlene threw our publicity staff into a dither immediately upon her arrival in the United States. Here was a glamorous and (on the screen) dangerous woman who in her first interview talked almost exclusively of her baby and her husband, Rudolf Sieber, a German director. There was some talk of asking her to avoid any further interviews.

This system had worked remarkably well for M-G-M with Garbo. At first the Swedish actress had been cooperative in publicity stunts, but, growing popular, had insisted that she be unaccompanied by a publicity man during interviews. M-G-M's publicity chief, Howard Dietz, had insisted to the contrary. Neither would budge, and therefore interviews were avoided. The result was the beginning of the legend of Garbo's silence, which proved more than satisfactory with all concerned—Garbo, the company, and the public.

A wall of inaccessibility erected by us around Marlene would have appeared to be an imitation of Garbo, which of course we were anxious to avoid. So Marlene talked about her baby or anything else she wanted to, and soon was considered a rival rather than an imitator of Garbo. As everybody knows, Marlene is today as devoted a grandmother as a mother, and as glamorous as ever.

Marlene's indifference to publicity was a major reason why millions of American women today wear slacks. At one point the publicity department decided that new press photographs of Dietrich were needed. Being in-between pictures, she did not feel like dressing up in fancy gowns for the sittings.

"I'm loafing around in slacks," she told Blake McVeigh, the publicity man assigned to get the pictures. "If you want to shoot me this way, all right."

That idea was rejected.

It happened that a little later McVeigh noticed a small display of gardening slacks for women in a Los Angeles department store. He thought, well, if even a few women wear slacks there might be an angle in Marlene's suggestion. She posed in her trousers and, to the surprise of everybody, the photographs were in great demand by the press. All over the country the stores were raided for their small supplies of women's slacks. The rage was on.

In Marlene's first picture for us, *Morocco,* in 1930, she was a dangerous woman endeavoring to turn Gary Cooper from his duty. Here, of course, was another indestructible player.

Gary Cooper has always been the solid, taciturn character off the screen which he has been on, a lover of horses and a great hunter. At the beginning he was not much of an actor. But he was a plugger. In any role given to him he did his level best. That is very high praise. His determination enabled him to climb to greater heights than most of the quicker talents ever attained.

Talking pictures brought new opportunities to stage players. Ruth Chatterton made many successful pictures for us. We brought the four Marx Brothers to the screen and they became almost overnight sensations. The stage training of Claudette Colbert, Fredric March, Kay Francis, Jack Oakie, and Jeanette MacDonald allowed them to rise swiftly. Older players such as Walter Huston, Charles Ruggles, and Frank Morgan soon registered high marks.

As for the motion picture industry as a whole, the coming of sound was a mighty lift. The expense of the change-over was far outweighed by the vast attendance increase.

21

THE depression, which was causing havoc in American and world business, at first did not affect the motion picture industry. It may be that people wanted to forget their troubles by going to a picture, and of course the "talkies" had been a big shot in the arm. At any rate, in 1930 the profits of the Paramount-Publix Corporation were $18,000,000, the highest ever. Our assets had risen in less than 2 decades from the practically none at the Twenty-sixth Street studio to $300,000,000.

People spoke of the motion picture industry as "depression proof." Yet I knew too well its hazardous nature to expect complete escape from the ills besetting others.

Sam Katz, the head of the theater division—we now controlled in the neighborhood of 2,000 theaters—had made a significant remark during a lecture at the Harvard Business School in 1927. "We can lose enough money on our theaters," he said, "to sink the Famous Players."

He was pointing up the fact that most of the money

paid by the public remains in the theaters, that only a relatively small part goes into picturemaking—therefore good business in the theaters could enormously swell our profits, which it had. Poor attendance could quickly engulf the production end, which it now did.

The year 1931 was not so good as its predecessor, yet profits stood at $6,000,000. Then the bottom dropped out. The loss in 1932 was a staggering $21,000,000. Paramount-Publix stock dropped rapidly. This was particularly embarrassing because in purchasing many of the theaters we had paid with stock which we had agreed to repurchase at a fixed high sum.

I did not go into details about the business operations on the way up, and I will not go into them on the way down. There were attractive offers for the purchase of the company. But I would not sell. It would have been possible for me to cash in my stock and retire with a large fortune to watch the debacle from afar. I chose instead to try to support the market. At last the stocks fell almost to nothing and certain creditors forced us into receivership. Some of these creditors and their representatives tried to push me out. Just as I would not sell out, I would not get out.

Stanton Griffis, who came to Paramount a few years later as chairman of the executive committee, remarked in his recent book, *Lying In State,* that the company's creditors "had bequeathed it a diamond-studded board of directors, made up mostly of railroad presidents, bank presidents and similar tycoons selected, so it seemed, for their complete ignorance of the motion picture industry."

There were some hardheaded financiers anxious to right the ship so that it might haul cargo in smoother post-depression water. There were others who wanted to put on gay yachtsmen's caps and shout commands. Some of the results were amusing, even though my laughter at the time was somewhat muted.

I recall one gentleman who, after gathering a large batch of claims, walked into my office forthright and informed me that he was taking over. I will not cause him embarrassment by using his name, which is not widely known to the public anyhow. I will describe the incident, however, since it shows a facet of the show business.

As I say, he came into my office one morning with a straightforward announcement that he intended to take over.

"All right," I said, rising from my desk. "Here you are. I must explain that a few decisions must be made today. Whether, for example, you will pick up Gary Cooper's option? It is a fairly important decision because it runs into six-digit figures. There are others of a similar nature. For example, the production budget for next season—"

The gentleman stopped me. "No, I can't hope to get a grip on things so soon. I was thinking of taking an office while getting my bearings."

"In that case," I said, "why not set up in my library? There you'll be close at hand to watch how things work."

He agreed. But he was restless and soon came back. "You have a studio over on Long Island, don't you? Any pictures being made?"

"Yes."

"Maybe I ought to run over there and size up the production end."

I checked the studio schedule. "Fine. Ben Hecht and Charles MacArthur are shooting today. I'll ask my son Eugene to take you over."

Hecht and MacArthur were famous for their shenanigans, and especially their irreverence for anybody from the business side suspected of wanting to interfere with whatever they were doing. These two would not provide the gentleman with the most dignified introduction to picturemaking. But in this case they were putting up their own money as independent producers under an arrangement with us for studio space and film distribution, and I thought they might at least ignore the intrusion.

Eugene telephoned in advance and then set out in a taxicab with the gentleman, hoping for the best. The moment he walked on the set he knew he wasn't going to have it.

Not a light was on, not a wheel was turning. Hecht and MacArthur sat in gloomy silence. A little distance away sat Jimmy Savo, an actor whose ability to register gloom was unsurpassed. He appeared to be expecting the world to end.

Eugene introduced the gentleman.

"I hope you will excuse us," MacArthur said courteously. "We are working very hard and in all fairness should not be disturbed."

The face of the gentleman was puzzled, seeing the

condition of the set, but he and Eugene found chairs and waited. Nothing happened for an hour or so.

Finally Hecht aroused himself. "We better knock off for lunch," he said.

MacArthur stirred slightly. "What do you suggest?"

"The Colony is all right with me," Hecht replied. "A secretary can have a waiter sent over to take the order."

The Colony, one of Manhattan's more expensive restaurants, if not the most expensive, lay two or three miles distant through heavy traffic. The extra expense would go to Hecht and MacArthur themselves, but the gentleman did not know it.

He could stand it no longer. "I think you might at least," he said, "order by telephone."

No one paid any heed to his remark.

"We have dignitaries visiting here," MacArthur said. "It seems to me that we owe it to them to serve champagne."

Hecht objected. "It wouldn't look good. We'd be sitting around drinking champagne while the crew drank beer."

"In fairness," MacArthur agreed, "we must order champagne for the crew as well."

Hecht nodded. "Might as well order lunch for everybody while we're at it."

After a while a waiter arrived by taxicab and took orders for thirty or forty persons. Some time later a caravan of station wagons appeared and the repast was spread. There was a great popping of corks and hearty eating. The visiting gentleman did not appear to enjoy his lunch.

At about two thirty Hecht and MacArthur decided to go back to work.

"First thing," Hecht said, "we better look at the Savo rushes." He turned to the gentleman. "We've got one of the funniest scenes ever filmed. You'll die laughing."

Adjournment was made to the projection room, a bottle of whisky ordered, and the projectionist was signaled. There were a few more interruptions, but at last the rushes were thrown on the screen. Jimmy Savo was observed stepping over a window sill into a room. That was all.

Hecht and MacArthur howled with laughter. They had the scene run over and over, and each time their glee reached a new height.

"Funniest thing ever made," Hecht said. "It was your idea, Charley, and it will go down in history."

MacArthur modestly disclaimed full credit.

By this time the gentleman had had enough, and, motioning to Eugene, he departed without a backward glance. The whole thing had, of course, been a gag.

He charged into my office and reported the affair with vast indignation.

"Yes," I said, "these things sometimes happen."

"They should not be *allowed* to happen."

"You're right," I said. "Now, if you are able to eliminate them it will be a wonderful achievement. I have been dealing with actors and actresses and directors and writers—all sorts of creative people—for a long time.

Never yet have I figured out a way to keep things like this from happening once in a while."

The gentleman disappeared and never again tried, so far as I know, to reform the show business. Others got in deeper and in the end were even unhappier.

Meanwhile we went ahead making pictures, and here I must pay tribute to another durable trouper, Mae West, for the powerful lift she gave us out of the depression mire. Neither the sweet ingénue nor the glamor girl fit the depression years. Mae did. She was the strong confident woman, always in command. And that was the real Mae. Except for her strength of character she would not have become the sensation she was—perhaps would never have appeared on the screen at all.

Mae had scored many hits on the stage as the embodiment of lusty sex. But picturemakers had shied away, not knowing exactly how to use her. Certainly no one believed that the Mae West of the stage could be transferred almost intact to the screen.

In 1930 we had, however, signed her for an important role in George Raft's *Night After Night*. Mae went to Hollywood but script trouble developed and she was idle for four weeks. When the script finally was ready, she refused it. She had always written her own material and this was not the Mae West of her creation.

While Manny Cohen was then head of the studio, Al Kaufman was one of his principal executives and Al was very disappointed. The wardrobe and screen tests had been fine. He had an idea that Mae would be either a terrific hit or a big flop, and the only way to find out was to take a chance. Everybody wrangled with Mae, including Al, but she wouldn't start the picture.

One night Al took Mae and her manager, Jim Timony, to dinner for a final appeal. It happened to be Mae's birthday, and, while she does not drink—or smoke either—it was a gala evening. Toward the end of it, Mae opened her handbag, took out a check, and handed it to Al. It was for twenty thousand dollars—her salary up to date.

"I'm leaving for New York tomorrow," she said.

Al had an idea.

"Mae," he said, "why don't you write the part the way you want it. Then come into the studio tomorrow. I'll get everybody together and we can make a test. We'll try the script the way it is now and then we'll try your way. If we like ours better, I guess you just take the train. If your way is obviously better, then we'll accept it."

"A deal," Mae said.

Next afternoon Mae was on hand with her script. The director put her through the paces in the manner he had expected to, and, a good sport and honest to the core, she did her best. Then she directed herself according to her own script and ideas. Plainly her own characterization was far the better. The public thought Mae knew what she was about too, for in *Night After Night* she stole the show.

Then came *She Done Him Wrong* based upon one of her own stage plays and for which she wrote the entire script. Mae's celebrated invitation in that picture, "Come up and see me some time," became as much a part of the depression era as the Sheik and "It" had been of the early and later twenties.

It seems to me that the incident described above portrays the true Mae West—honest, direct, extremely knowledgeable in her craft. I have not seen Mae for a while, but recently Al Kaufman was talking with her in Hollywood and mentioned my book.

"Anything I can do to help, I'll do," Mae said.

And she sat down and wrote an account of an experience which she had never related before. With many thanks to Mae, I print it below.

> Very few people know my secret ambition—to be a lion-tamer. It began when as a child my father took me to my first circus at Coney Island. Through the years I mentioned it very rarely and only to intimates. The response to my enthusiasm was mainly negative and uninspiring. People were incapable of understanding unless they themselves felt the same driving fiery compulsion I had toward lion-taming.
>
> Throughout my career whenever I was on the road with a show or making personal appearances I had myself driven around to admire the points of interest of each new city. I would always inquire whether there was a zoo, and if there was, it was the first place I would go. To this day I visit every zoo I can. My animal instincts, perhaps?
>
> At any rate, each new sight of the lions started a chain reaction in me which pulled my old lion-taming ambitions into top priority. I would stand before the lions' cage and see myself inside, in full command. And the

secret drive increased in power. There was no moment at the height of my success that I would not have gladly exchanged positions with any lady lion-tamer—for a limited time at least.

Finally I saw a way to realize my ambition. After my first starring picture for Paramount, *She Done Him Wrong,* the studio was eager to follow immediately with another. At a meeting with producers and executives I was told that they wanted my second picture to be big and expensive. What kind of a big and expensive story did I want to do? What would make me happy? They were anxious to make me happy and I was willing to let them.

This, I thought, is the moment I have been waiting for. Excitement began to take hold of me. I didn't show elation. Somehow I felt that to do so would frustrate my plans. So I was casual when I said, "Well, how about a circus story? You know—Madison Square Garden and all that goes with it."

And then I held my breath, waiting for the answer.

"Circus story?" an executive said. "Madison Square Garden? That means big sets, lots of people. That would cost a lot of money. Circus life is glamorous. It would be colossal."

Well, to me it was better than that. Out of the idea grew my second starring picture, *I'm No Angel,* the story of a glamorous lady lion-tamer. Day by day my excitement grew as I approached closer to the supreme moment of my life. I had no fear whatever. If lions are killers at heart, I do not recall ever thinking about the fact in relation to myself. Anyhow, my obsession with getting into the cage with lions had become so great that I could recognize no stop signal.

I had a talk with the trainer. He said that the lions he would use in the scene were well-trained and fairly tame. There was always some element of danger, he said, but he thought that I would be safe in the cage long enough to make the scene.

At last the great day came and I arrived at the studio bright and early. I hurried into my make-up and white lion-tamer's uniform—a gorgeous outfit of white silk tights, white boots, a white military jacket lavish with gold braid, a tall white military cap flaunting white plumes, and a military cape of ermine.

Thus arrayed I went into the Madison Square Garden set, accompanied by my entourage of maids, hair dressers, make-up artists and assistants. What a lovely day was in store for me.

After a delay of an hour or so, Wesley Ruggles, the director, told me that we could not shoot the scene as planned. Mr. Ruggles was looking very serious that morning.

"The head trainer isn't here," he said. "And there's no one to double for you. You should have a double. I always thought you ought to."

"Why," I said, "it was understood that I was to get in with the lions myself for a few shots. I don't need a double for what I want to do in there. You can take them going through their tricks with a double later on."

"But you don't understand," he said. "I didn't want to upset you, but the head trainer had his arm almost torn off this morning by one of those lions. We figured he could handle them while you were in there, but now he's gone. And the lions are restless besides."

What a let-down. This was terrible. I was grieved to hear of the accident, of course, and said so. But the old terrific urge was not to be downed. Not when the means of satisfaction was close at hand.

"Do you really need him?" I asked. "Can't we go ahead with the assistant trainer?"

Mr. Ruggles was positive. "I can't let you take a chance with those lions," he said.

In a few minutes my producer, William LeBaron, was sent for, and he arrived with two assistants to hear my story. He said it was a daring thing that I wanted to do and he agreed that it would make the picture a lot better. But even he couldn't commit himself.

Just then Al Kaufman came on the set. He was and is a reasonable and understanding man, but also an excellent business executive. He listened as I blurted out, "This lion scene is the main reason I'm doing this picture."

Al thought a moment, and then he told me that the studio had an enormous investment in me and this picture. Aside from the humanitarian feeling of not wanting to have me mangled or killed, the business risk of losing both me and the picture just wasn't to be taken lightly.

Finally Al said, "All right, Mae, I'll tell you what we'll do. Let's leave this scene to the last. We'll get all the rest of the picture shot and then we'll do the scene."

"Oh, no!" I protested. "You just want to put it off to the last moment, hoping I'll go cold on it. You don't want me to do it. We're ready now and I want to do it now."

I argued for a long time and finally they gave in. After lunch I returned to the set and things began to move.

The lions were driven out of the cage and the wicked lion who had hurt the trainer earlier in the morning was separated from the others. The cage was thoroughly cleaned from top to bottom. At last things were ready. They drove the lions back into the cage. Cameras were set up to get the scene from different angles. This wasn't something you could take over and over again.

Unknown to me, the studio had ordered men with guns loaded with live bullets to stand at vantage points outside the cage. They were ordered to shoot to kill if any of the beasts made the slightest move to attack me. I was confident of my safety, but apparently no one else was. The assistant trainer was not allowed in the cage, of course, because his presence would have ruined the scene.

Over the loud-speakers the ringmaster announced the act, and I made my entrance into the cage. The iron door clanged behind me and I was alone, facing the semicircle of lions. The crowd fell silent and tense as I began moving about, cracking the whip.

Ah, at last here were lions surrendering to my will. They looked at me with great big beautiful but dangerous eyes. They were fascinating to me and seemingly fascinated by this stranger in dazzling white and gold. They snarled, they pawed at me. If one of those immense thrown paws had reached me I very probably would not be writing this now.

In dominating them I experienced afresh that first vivid thrill when my father took me to see Bostick and his lions at Coney Island. Now the thrill was multiplied a thousand times.

Yet, curiously, I was not nervous or concerned for my safety. I do not call it bravery. It was something I can

> give no real name. Let's just say that this, and only this, was a fitting climax to the obsession which had driven me. I had to do it, and I did.

It is pleasant to know that Mae was not shaking in her boots. I can testify that others were shaking in theirs—as far away as New York City. The long-distance telephones were humming that day. Mae will grant, I think, that film producers have their bad moments.

22

PARAMOUNT climbed out of receivership and bankruptcy reorganization in 1935, still shaky, and started off anew. By this time I was in my sixties, had been working hard for fifty years, and was only too happy to look about for a younger man with a thorough knowledge of the show business to assume the heavy burden of the presidency in the reorganized company. We found him almost in our own home—Barney Balaban of Balaban & Katz, the Chicago theater chain which had been closely associated with us.

Barney was still under fifty, but having gone into show business as a kid, he had a quarter of a century of experience behind him. Barney is a soft-spoken man, deeply religious, a student of Lincoln and a collector of Lincolniana, and a tremendous worker who never seems happier than when his teeth are in a tough problem.

I took over the chairmanship of the board, usually a job with fewer day-to-day worries than that of the presidency. But as it happened our Hollywood production was not satisfactory. Jesse Lasky had given his all to stem the tide of disaster, and then, caught in the turmoil of the creditors' attack, had resigned to produce as an independent. Others had been tried as production chief but without the results desired. Something fairly drastic had to be done.

The board of directors had, as a matter of fact, employed Joseph P. Kennedy, the financier, to make a thorough study of Paramount. Kennedy's conclusion was that the company almost inevitably would slip back into receivership.

I volunteered to go to Hollywood and see what I could do. My wife and I naturally hated to pull up stakes and move to the coast, but she did not complain. What had to be done, had to be done, and as always she was by my side. We took a suite in the Ambassador Hotel in Los Angeles and hoped that events would justify our return home in a year or two.

Not long ago William Powell was recalling an incident which occurred soon after my arrival. One day when leaving the hotel dining room, I saw Bill and Jean Harlow at a table, and, not having seen either for a while, stopped to say hello. Some years earlier Powell had left us in a raid by another studio. Afterward he had suffered a run of bad pictures, with a box-office drop. Now the pendulum was swinging again.

"Bill," I said, "those *Thin Man* pictures are wonderful. I was never happier to see any one make a comeback."

Powell had made his mark originally with us as the heavy in *Beau Geste* and then had turned to leading man and comedy roles. He was always modest, good humored, and a hard worker—invariably one of the best liked men on the lot.

"We all expect to go down," he said, smiling, "and the most fun of all is to come back up."

"Very true," I said. "And, Bill, if you can make it, I can make it."

He and the lovely Jean Harlow wished me luck and I bid them good-by. It was the last time I was to see Jean alive. The tragic death of this beauty at the height of her career was a blow to all filmdom, and of course bitterest of all for Powell.

At the studio we had a fine group of stars. Mae West was piling one success on top of the other, to the surprise of those who had believed her good for two or three pictures at the most. Marlene Dietrich had accomplished everything expected, and more too. Now, with Garbo retiring, she held undisputed sway in the field of mysterious allure.

Claudette Colbert had entered pictures at the close of the silent era, and the one silent film she made had promised a bright future. For Claudette the arrival of sound was opportune, allowing her to take advantage of her starring Broadway stage experiences.

Among the other young ladies of great talent at the studio were Ida Lupino, Irene Dunne, Sylvia Sidney, and—just beginning—Dorothy Lamour.

Had the studio personnel taken a vote for "Queen of the Lot," doubtless Carole Lombard would have been awarded the honor. She was in her middle twenties at the time—incidentally, between marriages to William Powell and Clark Gable—and to me she recalled the Mary Pickford of the old Twenty-sixth Street studio. Like Mary, she was interested in everybody, whatever his or her station. Players vied to be in her films because she was likely to ask that their parts be fattened up rather than leaned down. The rank and file studio employees liked her because she was one of those agreeable people who manage to spread good feeling about.

Yet Carole, again like Mary, could be extremely demanding. She wanted a voice in her stories, in the choice of other players, in direction, and in many other things. She got it too, in a degree that amazed many other stars. The reason was that, like Mary, she understood production. She knew exactly what she was demanding, and why, and did not abuse any powers once granted.

Carole's death a few years later in an airplane accident while on a war-bond selling tour deprived the screen of one of its foremost comediennes, and was a heavy blow to thousands who had worked with her.

When one thinks of people easy to work with, Bing Crosby leaps into the mind. Bing has been with Paramount for twenty years.

I never close the door to my office, and recently I looked up and there stood Crosby. "Merely dropped in to shake your hand," he said, "and to say that everything has been lovely, just lovely."

It seems a curious thing, until one thinks about it, that we would not be able to cast Bing in the role of a man who has to be at work every day at a given time. The public simply would not expect Bing to get there. It was said of Douglas Fairbanks that he laughed and everybody felt good. In his pictures Bing takes it easy, shrugs off his troubles, and the audience feels the world can't be so bad after all.

Bing is, in fact, playing a part of himself, for he is good natured and the best of company. But he gets to work on the dot and is an extremely able businessman—possessed, some say, of a total-recall memory. After his representatives have come to terms on a contract, he glances over it with seeming casualness. People occasionally violate a small point in the fine print, just to hear him say, "Uh, uh! We can't do that."

Many who know Crosby intimately think of him, despite his affability, as basically a lonely man. He will be found late at night in some little hamburger joint, reading his paper, sipping coffee. He likes to dine at soda fountains. For a man with a famous face he has an amazing ability to conceal himself. He pulls his hat low, but not so low as to be conspicuous, takes a place against the wall if possible, turns a little away, reads his paper, and is seldom recognized by other than his friends.

In the middle thirties, when I was at the studio, Bing was teaming with Bob Burns in *Rhythm on the Range* and other pictures. Burns' homemade "bazooka" was, of course, to become additionally famous as a nickname for a weapon in World War II.

Among other male stars were W. C. Fields, Fred MacMurray, George Raft, Herbert Marshall, Jack Benny, Henry Fonda, Melvyn Douglas, and Frederic March.

The Hopalong Cassidy pictures were being made while I was in Hollywood. I cannot claim, however, to have had an inkling of their enormous impact on the future. Though turned out almost as fast as sausages, they differed from most westerns, and except for that difference the later television audiences might have had to get along without their Hoppy.

For my eightieth birthday celebration banquet in Hollywood, the committee had put together a number of clips from some old films. Lionel Barrymore spoke the narrative. "And there's Bill Boyd," he said at one point, "in *The Volga Boatman.*"

A black-haired lad came on the screen. Suddenly the film broke, in the manner of the old days. Upside-down reel numbers flashed as the projector ground to a halt. Bob Hope, acting as master of ceremonies, and Reuben Moumolian, in charge of entertainment, jumped to their feet as if in a panic and conferred about what to do while the film was being mended.

On the horizon a lonely horseman was espied. The music went up, the spotlights turned to the rear of the banquet hall, and lo and behold!—in rode Hopalong Cassidy on his white horse Topper. Bill Boyd lifted his sombrero from his now-white hair as with vast good-humor he rode Topper down the aisle. Then he turned, gave me a flourishing salute with the sombrero, and rode away.

The adventures of Bill Boyd as Hopalong Cassidy in real life are filled with more amazing twists and turns than any he ever encountered on the screen. But let us go back to the beginning.

The Hopalong Cassidy character was invented in a series of books by author Clarence Mulford for Doubleday & Company. A veteran producer, Harry Sherman, contracted for the picture rights and for several years unsuccessfully sought financing to make them. Sherman was out of the old school. At twenty-eight he had made a million dollars on a ten-thousand-dollar investment for rights to show D. W. Griffith's *The Birth of a Nation* west of the Mississippi River. After that he had concentrated on westerns starring Dustin Farnum, Jack Paget, Jack Holt, and others.

Sherman had eventually run into hard luck but I think had managed to produce one Hopalong Cassidy picture before Paramount financed him and took over distribution. Altogether more than fifty Hopalong pictures were made.

Sherman had wanted James Gleason to play Hopalong Cassidy, since in the books Hoppy was a slender, wisecracking type. He couldn't get Gleason and someone suggested William Boyd. Cecil De Mille had used Boyd as a juvenile lead in silent films, but now he was almost forgotten. Sherman finally located him at Malibu Beach, and Boyd worked himself into the physical shape necessary for a cowboy role. Sherman was struck particularly with Boyd's infectious laughter, which he thought would be very good for the role.

The Hoppy pictures had a formula—the old man, played usually by Gabby Hayes, the middle-aged man, played by Bill Boyd, and the lad of twenty or so, played by various young actors. It was a foursome if the white horse Topper is granted billing. The budgets were very low, but Sherman employed one of the best of the outdoor cameraman, Russell Harlan. And Sherman insisted that the pictures be made with great care.

In westerns it is possible to cut corners by making long shots of herds, riders in the distance, by shooting with infra-red film to simulate night scenes, and by various other devices. Sherman insisted on establishing character by bringing the players close to the camera, even though it was more expensive.

Boyd was more than happy to play close-up scenes, inasmuch as he had no particular love of the saddle. He learned to ride and do the other things necessary but he was not cowboy bred like Tom Mix or a western fanatic like Bill Hart. This was all to the good, for his urbanity was a pleasant new ingredient of the western film.

Sherman complained sometimes because Boyd did not especially like to meet people and would not go on exploitation tours except under pressure. Yet the money rolled in and everybody was happy.

Then the cycle ended. The public did not want to see Hoppy pictures any more. Harry Sherman called it a day and sold the rights to the films to a company which buys up old pictures for small sums on the chance of future salvage.

Now Bill Boyd cursed the day that he had ever become Hopalong Cassidy. He was typed. He had proved himself in sound pictures, and no one would hire him for a role because the audiences would say, "There's Hoppy."

Boyd put an advertisement in a trade paper which attracted considerable attention. "Don't rope me in," he pleaded with Hollywood. But it didn't get him a job.

Then television came along and everybody knows what happened. But here again there is irony. Why the great success of the Hoppy pictures? Because Harry Sherman had established character, had insisted that players be brought up to the camera. Therefore the pictures had real drama and humor—were not simply long shots of scenery and galloping horses.

Yet Sherman no longer owned a penny's worth of the pictures. Show business is full of tricks, many of them tragic. Sherman is dead now, but he was struggling to put a stake together for a comeback at a time the Hoppy pictures, which he had made with such great care, were grossing a fortune—largely because of that care.

Bill Boyd had made a few Hoppy pictures on his own as the cycle was petering out. Whether he still owned them I do not know, but the fact makes little difference. He was back. Large sums rolled in to him for endorsement of products and personal appearances. Now he is making pictures especially for television and I understand that the Hoppy products are in as great demand as ever.

There is one more twist in the Hopalong story. When the picture rights for the books and the name were first purchased, somebody—his identity has been forgotten—in Doubleday's subsidiary rights department tossed in all the rights he could think of, including those for television. At the time, no one thought much of television's immediate future, least of all Hopalong Cassidy's future in it.

But there it was in the contract. The author was struck by a fortune as if by a thunderbolt. He and the publisher share in all income from the vast Hopalong enterprises, down to royalties from the last belt buckle.

23

AFTER two years, with Paramount once more strong and climbing, I was able to finish my job as manager of the studio. In a long article about the company, *Fortune* magazine remarked kindly, "the improved product is attributed to sixty-four-year-old Adolph Zukor." To take over the Hollywood reins we chose Y. Frank Freeman, at the time head of the theater division. We could not have picked better, as things have turned out. A long-time exhibitor in the South—I had met him first in 1915—he knew the show business from the ground up, and at the same time was an astute and tireless executive.

And so at last, with that quiet dynamo Barney Balaban as president, and Frank Freeman ably commanding in Hollywood, I was able to take things easier. The qualification "easier" is necessary, for in the film industry there is no such thing as taking things "easy"—not and stay in front, which is the only satisfying place to be. Maintaining pace with or ahead of the competition is only a part of it. More important is to keep up with the public. And one never knows what new storm will necessitate a firm grip on the apple cart to keep it from upsetting.

The storms came, and all have not yet blown themselves out. But fair winds came too. We have been particularly fortunate in talent. The loan-out system, begun nearly forty years ago when I let Jesse Lasky have Marguerite Clark for *The Goose Girl,* has now to a large extent done away with the star identified with one studio. A picture may be cast with players from two or three or even half a dozen studios. Perhaps "rental" would be a more accurate term than the current "loan-out," since the price is often higher than the player's contract salary.

A number of stars are nevertheless identified in the public mind with Paramount—notably Bing Crosby and Bob Hope, both of whom ranked among the top five box-office grossers in last year's compilation by the *Motion Picture Herald.* And the team which topped the list, Dean Martin and Jerry Lewis, gained their screen fame with Paramount. Among the others who have done all, or the major part, of their film work at Paramount are Alan Ladd, Betty Hutton, Marie Wilson, William Holden, and Rosemary Clooney—a young lady for whom I predict a tremendous film career.

Bob Hope is another of those indestructibles I have talked about, a born showman who probably was as happy entertaining small audiences—and he spent many long years doing that—as he is nowadays entertaining millions. It is his big heart which carries him through his unbelievably heavy schedule of benefit and overseas troop performances. But the good fun he gets simply out of making people happy lightens the burden.

The fifth of a stonemason's seven sons, Leslie Townes Hope was born in England but moved with his family to Cleveland while a young boy. He took the name Bob because playmates were switching Leslie Hope to "Hopelessly." In high school he learned to tap dance, a fact which he did not forget after becoming a clerk in a motor company. When he heard that Fatty Arbuckle was coming to Cleveland for personal appearances—this was before the scandal—and needed a couple of acts to fill out the bill, he teamed with a friend and got a dancing job. It lasted two weeks and then Arbuckle landed them a job in a musical road show doing a blackface number. Hope also sang in a quartet and played the saxophone.

There followed lean years in vaudeville, with a move up the ladder after Hope turned to a line of patter. Then came success in Broadway musicals, on the radio, and finally an overnight screen hit in Paramount's *The Big Broadcast of 1938*, when he teamed with Shirley Ross to introduce the song *Thanks for the Memory.* Since then he has made more than thirty pictures for us, including, as nearly everybody in the world knows, the "Road"—to Morocco, Zanzibar, Bali, etc.—series with Bing Crosby and Dorothy Lamour.

Having gotten the feel of things with those thirty-odd pictures, Bob should be about ready to hit his full stride. He is holding open the date of my ninetieth birthday, he tells me, in case the banquet for my eightieth is repeated and he is invited to be master of ceremonies again.

The team of Martin and Lewis is a throwback to the grand days of Mack Sennett comedies. These boys are professional comedians because it's a living—and nowadays a very good one for them. But they would be comedians anyhow, for the true comic spirit is inside them. There are times, true enough, when the Paramount studios seem a bit formal for them, and one wishes for the old rough-and-ready Sennett lot to turn them loose in. But on the whole it is nice to have a touch of the good old days.

The story is that, comic spirit or not, it was misery that brought the lads together, and just in the nick of time. They were dying as singles—Jerry Lewis in a pantomime act to phonograph records, Dean Martin as a romantic ballad singer. The owner of an Atlantic City night club in which they happened both to be playing told each separately that he had better do something about his act. They discussed things and hit on the idea of having Lewis, playing an awkward waiter, mess up Martin's singing numbers. That proved a little better.

Still desperate, they began creating disturbances on the beach in the daytime, Martin even pulling the "drowning" Lewis from the surf. After a crowd gathered they drummed up trade by haranguing it on the good points of their act. By the end of the Atlantic City engagement they had improved their routine, and soon were moving toward the top of the night-club circuit.

Finally they made a smash hit at New York's *Copacabana.*

A film company offered Martin a job—it didn't want "the skinny one"—but he refused to break up the team. Finally independent producer Hal B. Wallis signed the team, brought them to Paramount, and they were tried first in Marie Wilson's *My Friend Irma.* The audiences promptly took to them and they were on their way.

To Martin and Lewis the making of a picture is a skylark. One of their major assets is ability to create spontaneous comedy between themselves, and often the best thing is to outline a scene, turn on the cameras, and let them go. Without the cameras they are every bit as wild, especially Jerry Lewis. He may not love to take a fall as much as Ben Turpin did. But a fall bothers him not at all if it helps a gag along.

One day Lewis was eating lunch in the studio commissary with Martin and other cast members when someone brought word that he was wanted on the telephone. Leaping up, he was in full flight by the time he had reached the center of the big room. As it happened, a producer, not his own, started to walk from his table, talking the while to an assistant. Lewis, coming even, took a forward fall.

He caught himself on his hands and was up in a flash, but paused.

"That was a nasty thing to do," he said, and dashed on.

Naturally the producer was confused. He didn't think he had tripped Lewis, and of course he hadn't. But it took him a moment to realize that Lewis, hurrying to the telephone, had seen the opportunity for a gag, and had taken it with split-second timing.

It is true that such playfulness can result in crises. There was the matter of Lewis' scooter. I suppose the gentleman escorted by Eugene to the Hecht and MacArthur production would have been shocked that a scooter could bring about a high-level conference, but it did—more than one.

The studio streets are quite narrow and therefore automobile traffic is frowned upon. Bob Hope gets from his dressing room to sets on a bicycle which carries a sign: "Bob Hope—Available for Parties, Clubs, Weddings." Martin and Lewis each bought a powerful motor scooter. And Lewis' exuberance outmatched the motor.

The word was soon out—Lewis is bound to hurt himself with his wild-and-woolly riding. What could that mean? Even if he were not seriously injured, production might be shut down. And nowadays a shutdown is an enormously expensive thing. Should we ask him to take it easy? That was simple enough because he meant no harm. But once on the machine his exuberance came out again and he rode as if it were a bucking bronco. Forbid him to ride it? Not a good idea.

The problem finally resolved itself—the scooter got out from under Lewis and gave him a bad spill, injuring a knee and an arm. Production closed down. More conferences.

It reminded me of something I ought to have told the gentleman of the Hecht-MacArthur jest—for high spirits one must sometimes pay with worry and even with money. The high spirits are nearly always worth the cost.

As for the storms, the one which had the most immediate shock was the Government decree in 1948 ordering that theaters be split from producing companies. Paramount's 1,400 houses in the United States were affected. On the advice of our general counsel, Austin Keough, who had steered us through the rough legal waters of the depression, we complied rather than go to the Supreme Court—which some other companies did without success. A separate corporation, United Paramount Theatres, was formed. The exhibition division had long since gone into the black, and last year United Paramount used part of its surplus cash to purchase the American Broadcasting Company.

Separation of production and exhibition was the final act in the "war" which started back in 1917 when the exhibitors launched First National. I had never believed that we engaged in monopoly practices, as the Government said. But the ancient fight had been against my wishes, and I could not now believe that separation would be disastrous.

Yet the distribution system built over the years was thrown into momentary chaos, and the task of Al Schwalberg, head of distribution, became far more complicated. Our theaters in Canada—the name there is still Famous Players—and elsewhere in the foreign market were not disturbed by the ruling. But George Weltner, our foreign-division manager, was having his troubles owing to the Iron Curtain, the freezing of credits, and the like.

And of course there was television. We were in it to some extent ourselves, having bought into the Dumont company as early as 1938, and we owned station KTLA in Los Angeles. Our expert in this and other technical fields, Paul Raiburn, who has a practical background of engineering, was also directing development of a television color tube and experiments with Telemeter, a coin device used for selling programs in the home.

Yet the plain fact was that television was hitting the box office. I was never basically discouraged, having complete faith in motion pictures and our ability to cope, as we always had, with new challenges. At Paramount we have what might be called our policy committee, since we have no formal name for it. This consists of myself, Balaban, Freeman, Raiburn, Schwalberg, and Russell Holman, who joined the company just after the First World War and whose specific job is to co-ordinate activities of the main offices in New York and the Hollywood studio.

The committee began to look hard for new ways to improve our film product. I have mentioned that Edwin S. Porter was experimenting with three-dimensional pictures at the old Famous Players studio nearly forty years ago. From time to time over the last couple of decades we had seriously considered making them. Our feeling had been that the public would not take to the green-and-blue spectacles required. Invention of polaroid glasses reduced this objection to some degree.

But we moved carefully, experimenting at the same

time with the wider screen and stereophonic sound, which would allow voices to emerge directly from the mouths of players wherever they were in the picture. When the time came for public demonstrations the audiences would tell us, as always, what they wanted.

Meanwhile we redoubled our search for the public's desires in story material. After a picture was made we were more sensitive than ever to the previews. In the case of the Crosby-Hope-Lamour *Road to Bali*, for example, we cut out an expensive water-ballet sequence because the preview audiences felt that it dragged, slowing the picture.

Since we can never do any more than put our best foot forward, we expended more energy than ever on promotion. Here I want to pay tribute to that dauntless race, the publicity men. Why none of them has written the story of their fascinating craft is more than I know. I have space for only a couple of the classic tales.

One of the most celebrated, partly because it is a commentary on a phase of the industry, deals with Bill Pine and Bill Thomas, now a producing team for us. At the time of the story they were publicity men.

To gain attention for a picture titled *The Green Parrot* they conceived the idea of sending green parrots to the film departments of newspapers around the country. Each bird would shout, "The green parrot, the green parrot," etc., until the news people were thoroughly impressed—according to theory, at least. To train the birds, Pine and Thomas collected them in a room and played a recorded voice repeating the desired phrase.

The birds proved to be good students, and at last they were packed to go on their mission.

Then somebody changed the title of the picture.

The Paramount Theatre in New York City was the scene of a press-agent stunt—the current term is "gimmick"—which is credited with boosting singer Frank Sinatra onto the high road, and with starting a debatable trend. The author of it was the late George Evans, who was representing Sinatra.

For the singer's first appearance on the Paramount stage, Evans hired ten or fifteen girls and scattered them through the audience. They had been instructed to begin screaming when Sinatra hit his first note. A couple of them were detailed to swoon. Evans hired an ambulance to arrive at the theater to pick up the swooners.

Sinatra began, the girls screamed, and those assigned to faint did so. And then something happened which Evans had not expected. Mass hysteria swept through *all* the teen-age girls present. Many swooned on their own volition, free of charge. Bona-fide ambulances had to be called.

Naturally the press stories were far bigger than had been expected. Sinatra's stock zoomed—and teen-agers continued to scream and to swoon.

A publicity man devoted to his trade dearly loves the "gimmick." But most of the work is hard plugging from the moment a picture is conceived. In the case of Cecil B. De Mille's *The Greatest Show on Earth,* for example, our head of publicity and advertising, young Jerry Pickman, an ex-Brooklyn Dodgers bat boy, set the drums rolling more than two years before its release.

Pickman reads all the original stories and keeps up with any changes in order to direct the publicity and the advertising, which is usually made up well in advance. A Hollywood staff under Teet Carle gets out stories about cast personalities and does its best to provide Hedda Hopper (a former Paramount featured player), Louella Parsons, Sidney Skolsky, Jimmy Fiddler, and the other film columnists with lively material. The New York staff under Herb Steinberg concerns itself more with the pictures after release.

Pickman sent his men with De Mille's crew when it first joined the Ringling Bros.-Barnum & Bailey Circus at its Sarasota, Florida, winter quarters in 1949. They stayed with the crew during the entire shooting. It may be that members of the publicity clan occasionally fear suspicions of their pronouncements, for they took affidavits from newspapermen who had watched Betty Hutton and Cornel Wilde performing on the trapezes.

De Mille is as meticulous about publicity as he is the making of his pictures. One day he was standing nearby while Herb Steinberg pointed out to a magazine photographer what he thought was a good angle to make a shot of Betty Hutton on a trapeze.

"How do you know?" De Mille asked.

"Well, I think it would be good," Steinberg answered.

De Mille motioned for a rigger's chair. "You won't know until you go up and see."

And Steinberg was hauled aloft.

De Mille was agreeable to Pickman's suggestion that Betty Hutton, Wilde, Jimmy Stewart—who played the clown—and others actually perform with the circus during the 1951 season. By the release date in early January of 1952 the expectations of the public were high.

We always know that a De Mille picture will do very well. But this one fooled us—by doing far better than we had dared hope. Its gross was twelve million, top for the year. The Academy Award it won for De Mille is a fitting tribute to the man I honor as the greatest showman of them all.

What of 3-D?

As I noted earlier, Edwin S. Porter was experimenting with three-dimensional pictures nearly forty years ago in our old Twenty-sixth Street studio. We had to put the project aside because of the press of solving the elemental problems of the flat silent screen. Every decade or so thereafter saw a flurry of experimentation.

We gave the matter a great deal of attention in the late thirties. Some visitors to the World's Fair in New York will recall viewing 3-D films there. Others who did will have forgotten. For, as we noted carefully at the time, the innovation stirred hardly a ripple of excitement. The public told us, in effect, that it was not ready for 3-D.

On an autumn evening in 1952 the public spoke up in the affirmative—and to me the tone was very positive. The event was the opening of Cinerama in New York City, on the night of September 30th. Cinerama is not three-dimensional, but the effect of bringing the audience and players together is much the same. The main excitement for me that night was the feel of the audience's tremendous response.

Variety asked me for a statement and I had this to say:

"I believe Cinerama is an opening wedge into the future. The possibilities are enormous, even greater than its developers are aware of. When we first started making feature pictures there were those who told us they wouldn't replace vaudeville. I am satisfied that Cinerama can be developed along the lines by which intimate entertainment can be shown."

I was speaking not so much of the technical Cinerama method as the intimacy of the audience and the players, however it might be gained. The wide screen and the strategic placing of loudspeakers had had much to do with getting the startling audience effect. Our experiments with wide panoramic screen and stereophonic sound were stepped up. We discussed 3-D pictures. But, frankly, we did not believe that patrons would wear the polaroid spectacles necessary for bringing the pictures into focus.

Then the public spoke again—quite urgently. Independent producer Arch Oboler had made a small-budget 3-D picture titled *Bwana Devil.* It was booked into the Los Angeles Paramount Theatre as a novelty, without high expectations. The public stormed the box office. Each day I eagerly awaited fresh box-office figures.

Every year around Christmas I go to Hollywood for two or three months to get the feel of production. When I arrived at the beginning of January, 1953, my mind was made up. In my speech at the banquet for my eightieth birthday I stated that three-dimensional pictures were the next big thing in the industry. I did more than make a speech, however. The other executives agreed with me and we went out on the set and halted the filming of *Sangaree*, a costume picture with Fernando Lamas and Arlene Dahl. Then we got an old stereo-camera with which we had been experimenting fifteen years ago up from the basement and shot the picture in 3-D with Technicolor.

At the same time we decided to unveil our wide panoramic screen and stereophonic sound. Our epic film *Shane* with Alan Ladd, Jean Arthur, Van Heflin, and young Brandon De Wilde was already completed, but our technicians were able to make changes so that it was suitable for the wide screen. That helped make *Shane* an even greater hit than we had anticipated.

Audience reactions to 3-D, the wide screen, and stereophonic sound have more than confirmed my general prediction made for *Variety*. Taken together, they are, in my considered opinion, a greater revolution than the "talkies" were.

The film industry is still in swaddling clothes. The great days lie in the future.

INDEX

Index

Index

Index

Index

Index